Reflections on the Mystery of Love

Reflections on

the Mystery of Love

by René Querido

RSCP

ISBN 0-945803-71-0

Printed in the United States of America

To my wife Merlyn
in celebration of having spent
more than thirty years together

Acknowledgements

Without the support of MariJo Rogers, this book could never have reached its completion. I am deeply indebted for the part she has played over the years.

The second part of the book would never have been completed without the invaluable help of Marion Van Namen, who gave not only immeasurable encouragement during my long illness but also made positive suggestions.

A special word of gratitude also to Judy Blatchford and Claude Julien.

R. M. Q.

Table of Contents

Foreword

This book is composed of two distinct parts, different in their composition and structure but united by the theme of love and human relationships. The first part contains the transcripts of three interviews recorded in 1996, during a visit by René Querido to Fair Oaks, California, subsequent to his retirement from the directorship of Rudolf Steiner College. The second part consists of a series of complementary essays that the author felt would enrich the sketchy and sometimes seemingly vague way the questions were formulated, and the answers given in the brief form typical of informal interviews.

This presentation keeps the freshness and spontaneity of the interviews intact. The tone is conversational, not academic. The interaction between the interviewer and the author has been left as it happened—whether it's a reaction, the clarification of a detail, or a further question. It is more a dialogue than a conventional interview.

The theme is approached gradually, in a periphery-to-center mode. Because human relationships do not take place in a vacuum, the build-up of a background was necessary before focusing on the theme. In the phenomenon of love between two people, appropriate conditions have to be met before it can happen . . .

Some answers seem to miss their marks, but a second reading will shed clarity or provide a spark for an inner feeling and point in a direction where answers can be found. These are answers to be pondered. In reading the text, one should avoid overreacting, and judgments have to be held until the substance sinks in. One more point of caution: These interviews were conducted towards the end of 1996, and as the world situation has radically changed since then, some facts seem passé and some answers irrelevant, but, paradoxically, this span of time serves as a remarkable indication of how forward looking and insightful Rene's answers were. For example, his remarks on the situation in Afghanistan were a clear prophetic sign of what was to take place later on.

It is with great joy that we are making these interviews and the complementary essays available now. We trust that the reader will understand our intent to render these texts as they have been written, with a minimum of tampering but with their authenticity and originality unchanged. We are grateful to René Querido for providing us with additional material to illuminate many aspects of the fascinating theme of love and everything else that surrounds it.

The Publisher

Part One
Interviews

First Interview
November 20, 1996
Fair Oaks, California

Q: *My first question concerns the soul: Where is the soul between death and a new birth, and is the soul eternal?*

A: The word soul is usually used rather loosely, but if you consider it from the point of view of Rudolf Steiner, then we have to differentiate between body, soul, and spirit. The physical body is transient; in other words we only use it for one incarnation. It is born and it dies. The physical body goes back to the elements. The spirit, which contains the I AM, is eternal, and for the eternal I AM to incarnate into the body, it requires a mediator. The soul is the mediator so it is not eternal; it accommodates that which is between the I AM and the physical body. If we speak about the soul, we speak about astrality and this also has something of the past in it. The soul carries our karma. Because the soul is not eternal, every child has to learn, every child has to develop his or her soul forces.

Q: *Does the soul reincarnate and why?*

A: In a certain sense the soul does not reincarnate, although that is what is commonly said. It is really the spirit that reincarnates. And why is there reincarnation? Because in one lifetime one can't perfect oneself to any considerable extent, only to some slight degree. Every incarnation, evaluated in the spiritual world after death, requires further enhancement, further development. In order to achieve this, we reincarnate.

Q: *How do we choose our new parents, from one incarnation to the other?*

A: The parents are chosen in such a way that with the help of the Spiritual Hierarchies our being tries to find the best possible accommodation, the most suitable and appropriate vehicle in order to express itself in this particular incarnation. So if, for example, a great musician reincarnates, then he or she will have to find a family in which the ear is especially developed. [For further reading on the Spiritual Hierarchies, see Rudolf Steiner's *The Spiritual Hierarchies and the Physical World* and *Spiritual Beings in the Heavenly Bodies and in the Kingdoms of Nature.*)

Q: *How many years does it take before we reincarnate?*

A: That depends. One can say on the one hand, that we have a male and a female incarnation once every 2160 years, but things have changed considerably. There has been an acceleration because the world is different as far as technological development is concerned—the wide ranging use of the car and the plane, and also the totally different configuration of the great cities of the world. That used to be the situation in the past and now there can even be a reincarnation within ten to fifteen years after death, as in the case of a victim of a violent crime, or in a war, or in an accident.

Q: *That quickly?*

A: That quickly, yes.

Q: *The Spiritual Hierarchies help us to reincarnate and to choose our new parents. Do they also help us to choose our attributes, and if they do, in which ways do they help us?*

A: After death we meet the Hierarchies—in other words we go through the Moon, Mercury, Venus, and Sun, right up to the Saturn sphere. In each of these spiritual realms—the orbit of each of the planets—is also the place where a particular Hierarchy dwells. That means that, as we go after death through the Hierarchies, we give back to them what we have been able to do on earth in a spiritual form. Then, when we return after the Midnight Hour, which is the turning point when we begin the process of reincarnation, the Hierarchies will grant us what we deserve, in a certain sense, for our new life on earth. We receive different qualities from different spheres. Rudolf Steiner gives us the example of Victor Hugo who had the task of being a very remarkable poet and novelist of an historical type. He received a particular impulse in the Saturn sphere. The wisdom of Goethe has its origin from the time he dwelt in Jupiter. One can look at great individualities who received from each of the Hierarchies special gifts on the way down. This throws a great deal of light on the gifts and talents that we are born with.

The Hierarchies & the planets

Seraphim		
Cherubim		
Thrones	—	Saturn
Kyriotetes	—	Jupiter
Dynamis	—	Mars
Exusiai	—	Sun
Archai	—	Venus
Archangels	—	Mercury
Angels	—	Moon

Q: *What is the role of our Guardian Angel? In which way does our Guardian Angel help us glean our attributes between death and rebirth? Which specific qualities do we receive from each of the Hierarchies?*

A: The Guardian Angel really accompanies us through all our incarnations. Each one of us has a Guardian Angel, or an Angel. We usually speak of a "Guardian Angel" in early childhood and youth. Later on we call them "Angels" and many people lose their connection with their Angel when they are in their thirties, but one can find it again at any time; that depends on us.

This Angel has recorded all of our deeds of the past, knows what we are doing now, at this very moment, and also what we still have to accomplish in the future. It is with the help of our Angel that also we go through the Hierarchies.

The different Hierarchies provide us with different qualities; many ancient traditions throughout the ages speak of the ninefold Hierarchies, usually divided in three groups, seven of which are connected with the planetary spheres, and the upper two realms with the Zodiac.

Upon descending from the Midnight Hour, the incarnating soul passes through each of the planetary spheres in succession. We might say that the dwelling place of the Thrones encompasses the orbit of Saturn. It is especially here that we receive powers of concentration, which can lead to a depth of understanding, for instance in wide historical vistas, also in research. Saturn is the planet of earnestness. Rudolf Steiner characterizes Victor Hugo as having received a great deal from this sphere. On earth, we find that he wrote monumental works, including *Les Miserables, The Toilers of the Sea,* and he envisaged writing a complete history of the human race in poetic form. He completed three volumes entitled *The Legends of The Centuries.*

In passing through the Jupiter sphere, which is the dwelling place of the Kyriotetes, we can be endowed by an overall sense of wisdom in earthly and spiritual affairs. Jupiter is embracing, cosmopolitan, but also jovial, and provides us with an interest in everything around us. Rudolf Steiner gave as an example a genius such as Goethe, who was endowed with strong impulses from this sphere.

The Mars sphere, which is the realm of the Dynamis, endows us with strong impulses of initiative. Great innovators, explorers, inventors, worldwide travelers, and also conquerors have received forces from this realm. That it need not always refer to an outer activity is epitomized by Rudolf Steiner's example that the critical, satirical, French author Voltaire received inspiration from this sphere.

The Exusiai, or Spirits of Form, dwell in the orbit of the Sun. Radiance and musical gifts are particularly associated with this sphere of harmony. Mozart might serve as an appropriate example of a being who received much from this realm.

The sphere of Venus is the dwelling place of the Archai, who can provide the soul with a sense of beauty, both inwardly and outwardly. These gifts also show themselves in all artistic activities. Certain poets have received inspiration from this sphere where also love is at home.

The Mercury sphere is the dwelling place of the Archangels, beings who, among other activities, are the folk-souls, gathering peoples according to language and cultural traditions. It is also the sphere of healing. Physicians and all those involved in therapeutic arts have received inspirations on the way down into incarnation from this sphere. We also recall that Mercury, named Hermes by the Greeks, is the god who is able to connect the heights of the divine with the depths of the earth. Its activity is to bring balance and harmony between extremes.

Finally, the Moon sphere, which is the dwelling place of the Angels, closest to the earth, is the entryway for a soul in its process of incarnation. It provides us with a certain reflective activity—the moon quite literally reflects the light of the sun, but has no light of its own—an ideal condition for reporters and journalists, those who have a genius for recording events. It is also associated with mobility.

This, of course, is a very sketchy description of a lofty process that would require a much longer treatment if we were to attempt to do justice to the mystery of this descent, which applies to every single human being before birth.

How much or how little we can receive from the different Hierarchies will depend on our previous incarnations. We should consider the question, what have we been able to give to the Hierarchies after death as a result of our life on earth? This in turn will determine what we can receive. It is quite clear that in mentioning Victor Hugo, Goethe, and Voltaire, we are dealing with exceptional human beings who are destined to play important roles in the cultural history of mankind. But the principle holds good for every human being; all of us have received some element in tune with our karma and the tasks that we are destined to fulfill in our relationship with others. Every profession, every vocation, every activity has meaning and this is also true of the simplest and least conspicuous. We are touching here upon the deepest mysteries of karma.

Q: *How does this apply to an ordinary person?*

A: We all have gifts but they may not be as strongly developed as in a genius. We do not only receive one, but several. Some of these gifts we can't receive because we are not sufficiently in tune, you might say, with the source of the giving that is bestowed by a particular Hierarchy.

Q: *How can we develop a healthy and appropriate relationship with the Hierarchies?*

A: It is most important in our time to renew our connection with the Hierarchies in an age when we have lost a true picture of the human being as body, soul, and spirit. As early as 869 A.D., at the Council of Constantinople, the spirit was eradicated by the church from the human trinity (it was decreed that the soul has certain attributes of the spirit, but that the spirit did not exist independently). The soul suffered a similar fate in the nineteenth century by Freud, who virtually denied the existence of the soul. For millions of people, the human being is reduced today to having only a physical body, and being devoid of any supersensible member.

To understand the working of the Hierarchies in the cosmos and in ourselves, the first step is to cross an inner threshold where once again we begin to experience the reality of the Angels in our destiny. We can then rise to the imagination of Archangels and Archai and gradually climb a ladder of deepening consciousness. Just as we have the kingdoms of nature around us—animal, plant and mineral—so, above us we have the three Hierarchies that comprise the nine spheres. We share in their existence just as much as we depend on the three kingdoms below us (mineral, plant and animal) for our food and existence.

Q: *Are the twelve constellations of the Zodiac also involved in that process? What contributions do they bring during the descent into incarnation?*

A: Oh yes, absolutely, one can put it like that: The signs of the Zodiac form our stature, our physical stature. For example, the chest part of our body is formed by Leo, the Lion. The head part of our forehead is formed by Aries; the inner organs are formed by Virgo and so on. The outer aspects of our being—the shaping, the sculpting—is formed by the Zodiac, whereas the inner organs are formed by the planetary spheres.

The Zodiac Circle and the Human Being

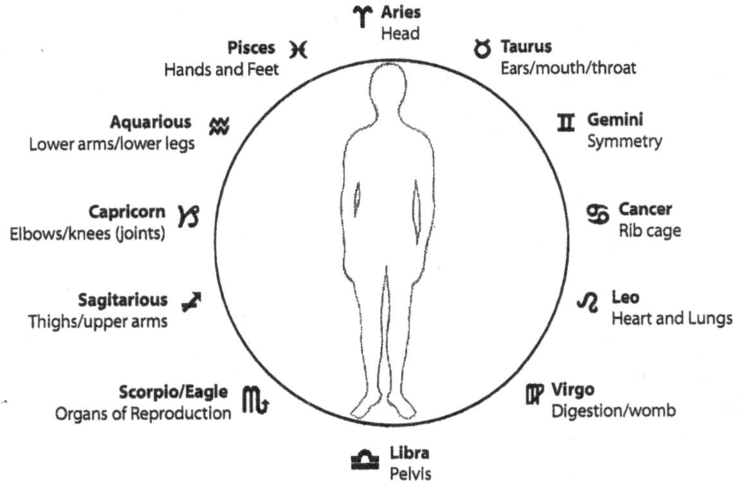

Q: *Are there any influences, attributes, or modifications that the eternal I receives from the planets, the Hierarchies, and the Zodiac?*

A: That is a profound question! One would have to approach it in the following way: Each human being has an I AM. Now, thirty or forty years ago one used to call that the Ego. Today one feels a little bit uncomfortable because we have expressions such as "an ego trip," and the Ego today in modern English usually refers to the lower self, but there is a higher self and to give it a name, we can call that higher self the I AM. That is our spiritual part, eternal and indestructible. The I AM is not static; in other words, it gains, if our life on earth was meaningful and we accomplished something of our destiny down here. When we die, the I AM is enhanced through the soul by what we experienced on earth. Gradually, in most cases, we advance, we don't fall back—and why do we wish to advance? Because we want to become, little by little, better servants of the Christ. Because the Christ in a certain sense encompasses in His being the totality of all the I AMs. We are members in Him. Each one of us has a part of the Christ in us, in every single one of us. The question is whether a human being becomes aware of that in the course of time or not? We can also fall back. The I AM can be diminished in quality through all sorts of stupidities that one does during one's lifetime, especially if we kill people, or if we do dreadful things that are not really in tune with the positive development of humankind.

Q: *The Angels and the Hierarchies seem to perform a minimal task! Is it just to evaluate and maybe to help us see more clearly during the time between death and a new birth?*

A: This is right. I think they don't intervene as such, but they record; they are the witness of our growth or of our sliding back.

Q: *This Ego had an origin, a beginning. When was it and how was it?*

A: We were created in the image of God.

Q: *Was the act of creation of the human being simultaneous with the creation of the animal, plant, and mineral kingdoms?*

A: Humanity was created long long before the mineral world, the plant world, the animal world. We were created spiritually first but we didn't incarnate until much later. So, the other realms—if you like, the other kingdoms—they incarnated first and we incarnated last, which is exactly the opposite of the usual theory of evolution. You see, the theory of creationism brings the picture that the human being remained in the spiritual world until the other kingdoms had been established and then we came down, so to speak, on the basis of the mineral, vegetable, and animal kingdoms.

Q: *So, is it just the reverse of the contemporary understanding of evolution?*

A: It's just the reverse! But we do have some of the animal in us, and we have some of the Angel in us. There is an interesting French expression that illustrates that relationship: *L'homme n'est ni l'ange ni bête et celui qui fait l'ange fait souvent la bête.* [Man is neither angel nor beast, and he who tries to be an angel often makes a fool of himself.]

Q: *Would you say that the animals have been created from us, and then the plants from the animals, and the minerals from the plant kingdom?*

A: Exactly! The whole evolutionary sequence is the other way around.

Q: *Do we choose our etheric body during our stay in the spiritual world or is it the consequence of how we have behaved with our physical body on earth?*

A: I am not sure whether we can say that we choose. The choice is not ours. I would put it like that: The choice is determined out of the past. For example, if a person has been very loving, very helpful to others in one incarnation, then in the next incarnation he or she might have a very good ether body, a healthy ether body.

Q: *Does what we eat, or how we live on earth, have an influence on our next incarnation?*

A: Absolutely! Yes, very much so. But it will never be a sort of insurance. The thing is that if you think, "Now, I'm going to do a lot of good so as to have an easier life next time"—that is not how it works.

Q: *"Brownie points" are not valid, they don't count . . .*

A: No, but one can put it this way (I'm coming back to the former example): If one has been loving and helpful in a previous incarnation, then in the next one, one might give a great deal of joy to people, but that does not mean that one's own life will be any the easier. There will be some radiance, there will be some help that comes out of that, but no personal gain, really.

Q: *What if we have been bad, if we have committed some reprehensible act, how is our etheric body affected?*

A: As a result of negative deeds in a previous incarnation, both our astral and etheric bodies will be affected. One person might be overly emotional, and another unable to relate to his feelings. These are of course extremes in the astral configuration. People given to habitual lying and deceit will be affected in their ether body, weakening their own life forces as a result. They may be unable to fit into society. People reject us, because they feel that we are not really in tune with them. There are many children also, and that is very sad, that are not liked in school by their peers. In Waldorf education, one would have to do everything one can to help such children understand and behave in such a way that they are liked. They might also be very lonely souls; they might be souls who just go their own way without any reference to anybody else—loners.

Q: *What about the astral body? Is it not so that the astral body feels the nature of our deeds that are then imprinted upon the etheric body?*

A: We should differentiate between the etheric body and the astral body, which records and carries our emotions, feelings, passions, aspirations and longings—in other words a quality of soul—and which we have partly in common with the animal world. The etheric body, or the body of formative forces, is responsible for our growth, our life forces, and our memory. We share our ether body with the plant world. Both these bodies or members of our being are invisible, and yet we can experience that they are part of us.

Q: *How is our astral affected by our stay in the spiritual world, the Hierarchies, and by all the influences that you have stated? Does it get improved, rejuvenated, refreshed?*

A: Upon our death, we leave our physical body behind and the etheric body dissolves in a short time, roughly three days. We see this etheric body that contains our memory forces, we see it as a great tableau that gradually vanishes. Through our own astral body that is still there, we go backwards over everything that we have done, from the other side. In other words, not what I have done to him or her but what he or she has felt because of my deed. So, if I have given a blow with my hand to someone—perhaps I had a certain satisfaction that I did it—but the point is: after death I have to repay and I have to feel the pain that I have inflicted on the other person. That is *kama loca,* or Purgatory. And during *kama loca* what happens in the feeling sphere is: "My

Goodness! . . . All these things that I have done—I've got to compensate for them. This is not my better self; this is not my loving self. I've done terrible things to a number of people. Whether I did them knowingly or not is not the point, but I did them." That journey backwards takes about a third of our life. If a person dies at sixty, then one third—which is twenty years —will be spent going back over our experiences. It corresponds to the number of days that we have slept. It's another way of looking at it.

Q: *If we sleep an average of eight hours a day . . .*

A: Right, on the average it's eight hours, so it's a third, that is how we come to a third. It's really that which is evaluated. The evaluation doesn't come through a terrible God or anything like that. It comes through ourselves. We realize what we have done and we sense it, we feel it—and that is being arranged in the moon sphere. There, already, there is a longing: "Oh Gosh, I've got to put this right!" But I can't put it right straight away because I have not got a physical body anymore. I haven't got the instrument. We have to live with that, for a very long time still, until next incarnation when we can put things right. There are of course, many variations.

Q: *To acquire this instrument that we spoke of earlier, does it take from the moment we die to the morning of the next incarnation or is there a moment when we are ready and just wait for the appropriate parents, for the right opportunity?*

A: No, I don't think so. I think that there is still a tremendous amount to be done first, because we have to go through the other spheres—Mercury and Venus, Sun, Mars, Jupiter, and Saturn— before we can reach the Midnight Hour. And now we have to reincarnate, and all those aspects that we have given to the spiritual world have to be evaluated, to be corrected, to be enhanced, so that our next life will be fruitful in compensation and further development.

Q: *Where or when is the set-up done for the situation we are going to encounter on earth in our next incarnation?*

A: That depends on the other people, because we have to meet them again.

Q: *Are we meeting the same people?*

A: Yes, by and large. There are exceptions, of course.

Q: *Can you explain?*

A: There is old karma and there is new karma. Old karma we can sense very easily when we meet someone and we feel tremendous sympathy or antipathy at first sight. That is a sign that it's old karma.

Q: *Whether negative or positive?*

A: Right! It is very strong either way. You get attracted to someone or you feel "I can't stand that person!" And new karma reveals itself when early impressions are lukewarm. You meet someone and they don't affect you all that much. But in the course of a certain number of weeks or years, you get used to them and so on. You begin to appreciate them perhaps, and that is a sign of a new karma.

Q: *How do we choose our new parents?*

A: That will depend also on our previous incarnation. The point is that, round about the age of thirty to thirty-three, we actually meet people who were either our parents in a previous life or are going to be our parents and relatives in the next life.

Q: *If one is attentive in this incarnation, can one can get a sense for this?*

A: Yes, one can get a sense of who will be his or her parents in the next life.

Q: *Are they people of influence, are they our friends, are they family members?*

A: It can be anybody. To begin with, we meet with our sisters, brothers, and parents of our previous incarnation round about thirty to thirty-three.

Q: *Doesn't that situation correspond to the third panel of the Foundation Stone: Practice Spirit Vision?*

A: Oh yes, definitely! These things are very subtle when you think of them really. One can make terrible mistakes. For example, you fall in love with someone at that time, and you even get married, and fundamentally that was a relative of yours in a previous life! It didn't require a marriage now.

Q: *How can one know?*

A: You find out. Life experience!

Q: *How can that new etheric, that new astral, and that new physical body—because they are new —how can they now match that eternal Ego?*

A: They are not entirely new. The physical certainly is, but the etheric body also carries aspects of our former etheric body, possibly of former incarnations. And the astral body also carries many aspects of our former lives, of former astral bodies. This is also true when you think of great individualities; they can carry over the etheric and astral of previous incarnations. For the common man or woman, it is much less, but nevertheless there are aspects of the past that play in.

Q: *What are the circumstances that allow a soul to incarnate again when it recognizes the parents or feels that it is the right opportunity? How does one know?*

A: The thing is extremely complicated, isn't it? Rudolf Steiner gives us a description that is not easy at all—that it is the child, in other words the I AM, that wishes to reincarnate, that brings the parents together. It happens in the parents through the eyes, to begin with. You see one another, you fall in love, and as a result of that which is passion, desire and the other things that play into it, that leads to the child being born. So the child loves the parents before the parents love the child.

Q: *Can we say that the child loves the parents before the parents love each other?*

A: Yes, as well. And the children might even—with the help of the Angels—bring people together. Because the unborn children swirl around, looking for a way in.

Q: *Can you speak about the hermaphrodite nature of man and woman, before the separation of the sexes?*

A: One can describe this as follows: During the first phase of the Lemurian age, there was no sexuality. In that sense there was only man/woman, woman/man and both were in one body, both man and woman. So of course procreation took place in a different way from the way it does now.

Q: *How?*

A: That's very difficult to say. It was not a sexual procreation, let's put it that way. It was perhaps more like a plant. And what happened then in Lemuria was the separation of the sexes. So, we were turned towards one another. Before we were back to back, so to speak. We couldn't look at one another and now we were turned around—we could see one another. There was also a split, in the sense that the woman, who is more spiritual, didn't descend quite so deeply in her physicality and man, the male, fell more deeply than he should have done. And now, from this time on, the act of procreation took place in the meeting of the two. Meeting of one partner who has not descended so far in the physical and another partner who has descended too deeply. In a female incarnation, the human being does not descend as strongly into physicality as a man. That is why she is more in touch with the divine world, and with her own deeper intuitions. This accounts, in an interesting way, for the fact that women are more readily attracted to spiritual and religious groups. Men tend to be more critical, less in touch with the intuitive, emotional side of their being. In a male incarnation, one falls more deeply into matter. Hence the need for incarnating during one lifetime as a woman and the next as a man in order to complete the experience of life on earth. So, there is always between a man and a woman that situation. That is why women are much more sensitive to the spiritual world unto this day, and men are more active in the physical realm and find it more difficult to recognize the spirit. But, if the marriage—if the meeting—of man and woman is right, then she can help him not to fall too deeply and he can bring her down a little, so she doesn't float off, if I may put it like that.

Q: *In the Bible it is said that the woman was ceated out of the rib of man: what does that mean?*

A: That is a picture, of course. I don't think we should take it literally. It has really to do with the heart forces, with the middle realm. Notice now, that God created woman out of the middle part of the human being. Not out of the lower part, not out of the limbs, not out of the head, but out of the middle realm, that is the realm of love, the heart.

Q: *Would you say that because of this origin, women are more sensitive in the realm of feelings, and therefore have maybe more astrality, more connection, and more understanding of the astral?*

A: Yes. Of course they do. Women are more in touch with their feelings, their emotions.

Q: *Is it true that during the two first months of gestation we are bisexual, that the sex is not really differentiated? Is that a continuation, a follow-up of the hermaphrodite aspect up to this day—and, if so, why?*

A: That's a good point! Because one can also say that during the embryological period we recapitulate every phase of the whole of humanity. That is a very important principle that there is always repetition. For example the child, once he is born, repeats all the stages of humanity. Already in the uterus we repeat the different stages of Saturn, Sun, and Moon and so on—but of course telescoped, in a very much shorter time. Nevertheless we go through those stages. Sexuality actually comes as the last thing that is determined in the descent toward the earth. A closer study of evolution will show that two principles are always interweaving. We should try to understand them in a musical way. On the one hand there is recapitulation, repetition, and yet there is always change, transformation, enhancement. Friedrich Nietzsche (1844–1900) spoke of the eternal return of the same. This is a great fallacy and would, of course, imply that "nothing new can happen under the sun." This can only lead to the uttermost pessimism. However, it will be equally erroneous to suggest that everything is new at every time and that there is no recapitulation, or repetition, out of the past moment in time.

Q: *We spoke of male or female incarnation; what does that mean? Do we have five incarnations in a row, of the same gender, or an alternation—and if there is an alternation, why?*

A: Usually it is alternated. A male incarnation calls for a female incarnation and vice versa. It alternates because we are only one half of the human being actually, but we have the other half in us. Every man has a female aspect and every woman has a male aspect. That is true, but the reality of meeting the other gender is far more important than meeting the other part of oneself, or rather it is equally important. A man should become conscious of his femininity; a woman should become conscious of her masculinity. But in the meeting of another person, that is where the karma really lies. You can't have karma with yourself!

Q: *That does not completely answer the question of regular alternation. I have heard you say that sometimes we have two or three incarnations of the same sex in a row?*

A: As you know, in French grammar there are always rules and then there are exceptions—and the point is that evolution is like French grammar. I really mean that quite seriously; there are so many rules and then there are about as many exceptions, so we could say, "that is the general rule, but. . . ." It can happen that an individuality has to reincarnate again and again as a man, not usually as a woman.

Q: *Why not?*

A: Because the man has to be active on the earth. He has to anchor himself to earthly things more strongly and that depends on the task of the individuality. But we can't incarnate more than seven times in one gender and then we have to change. Seven is the maximum, then we have to have an incarnation in the opposite sex, but that is an exceptional situation.

Q: *Can you talk about man having a female etheric body and vice versa?*

A: That is extremely difficult but we can try to approach it. What is the difference between male and female? The male is more active, the female is more receptive; that is a fact, isn't it? So, if we look at the act of procreation, the man with his organ becomes active and the woman receives what the man ejaculates, if we think of it purely physiologically. That is only a picture of what is happening at all levels, not only at the level of procreation. It is usually men who are inventors, not women. There are exceptions, for example Madame Curie, but try to tell me another one. You will find it difficult. If we had to do something in the world, until now we had to have a male incarnation, but now it is not quite like that. We have women statesmen, we have a Margaret Thatcher, we had a Golda Meir in Israel, an Eva Perón in Argentina. You can find quite a lot of woman who have leading positions. So, what are we really talking about? We are talking about activity and passivity, activity and receptivity. One would need a female incarnation if you have to be more receptive, more sensitive. Bearing children is also a receptive activity. Being a witness of what is happening into the world is receptive, but going out into a battle, struggling outwardly, is more active.

Q: *What kind of a battle do you mean—physical battle, or language, or any type of battle?*

A: Any battle! Yes. That is a way of looking at it—in business, in an army, in the academic world, in a number of professions.

Q: *Does that really affect the nature of man and woman in terms of relationships?*

A: It does—but the trouble is, in our own time there is a sort of mix-up that neither men nor women really understand their tasks anymore. There is a marked tendency for men to become female, in a certain sense. Some men like to let their hair grow and stay home, and many women have short hair and pursue their career and earn the family livelihood. The roles are upside down. Now, some people say: That is the equality of the sexes. It may be, but one has still to ask oneself: Is that going to work in the long run? And, in many cases it doesn't work that well! . . . Of course, it is very good for men to practice the art of looking after children, of feeding them, of changing babies' diapers; that is very good!—and for women to go out in the world, to have a position as vice-president in an insurance company, for example. It may also work well, but is that really what is needed? Do you really have to express it in a physical form so crassly? Can't it be expressed more in a soul form?

Q: *Is it only a question of the culture of our time, or do you see that more as a natural inclination given to man and woman?*

A: Well, I do think that it's a sign of our civilization, and particularly of the West. We are really talking of Western civilization—Europe, North America; we are not even talking of South America, because things are different, as you know.

Q: *Would you say that they are more advanced than we are, in a certain sense, or that they have kept on the track and we have derailed?*

A: No, they are still protected by a certain tradition.

Q: *Is that tradition valid for our time?*

A: For those people who live there, it is valid. If you go to Mexico, there are some wonderful things. If you go to Hawaii, and see how the Hawaiians live, there is still something traditional that works in a beautiful way. It's of course out of the past, I agree, and yet it's valid. Our whole civilization is attacked today by Ahriman. And Ahriman is doing quite considerable damage in men and women who are not understanding anymore their own place or their own relationship to themselves. But, that is a very big subject, isn't it? Then, one shouldn't forget that certain countries are turning to Islamic fundamentalism. Afghanistan just recently was in the news, and we find that the fundamentalists are taking over. The women have to wear a veil, they are kept behind bars, behind doors, they can't come out in the street anymore, they can't go to the universities, and all that sort of thing. The separation of man and woman, as you find it in Arab countries is another distortion. That is actually not what should happen either. The true task of man and woman is distorted in our civilization.

Q: *You have characterized what women shouldn't be doing, but what should they really be doing? Is the role of women only to bear children and to take care of the house, to be the servant of men? I am not talking of women now, but of men, as potential women in future incarnations?*

A: No, not at all. I think that one of the healthiest things that could happen to women is to become statesmen and rule countries. If there was a great number of women in important positions, they would bring soul, they would bring feeling, they would bring greater compassion and understanding to the affairs of the world, they would bring culture and civilization, for instance. The men have sunk pretty low, as far as modern culture is concerned, and there are many things that are not particularly healthy. Of course, you can say that there are boxing matches between women, but that is rare. In other words, violence is much greater on the part of men collectively and individually than it is with women. So, if women could really be appreciated by men they would have functions in a government or become the president of a country. You remember that in Israel we had Golda Meir, and there was Benazir Bhutto in Pakistan—although there were problems there—but be that as it may, I think that the influence of women in positions of responsibility can be wonderful as long as they don't turn into men—Margaret Thatcher in

England, for example, who became almost like a man. Women are keepers, protectors not only of the home but of civilization, of culture, of tradition.

Second Interview
November 21, 1996
Fair Oaks, California

Q: *Could you speak of the seven levels of love?*

A: Earlier on we have mentioned that the Greeks seem to have certain insights into the different levels of love. We recall that *eros* (erotic love) was a level that concerns especially the physical and the etheric, one might say. *Philia* is the level of friendship, and *agape* denotes spiritual love. If one considers that, and tries to see it in a modern setting, we might even venture to arrive at seven different levels of love, in accordance with the teachings of Anthroposophy, which can help us to conceive of a ladder of love related to the different parts of our being.

The Seven Levels of Love

Negative aspect		Positive aspect
egoism/abstraction	ATMAN	sacrifice
illness/destruction	BUDDHI	redemption/healing
stagnation/apathy	MANAS	revelation
alienation/estrangement	I AM (EGO)	recognition
disharmony/rejection	ASTRAL	desire/passion/harmony
indifference/isolation	ETHERIC	affection/tenderness
coldness	PHYSICAL	warmth

Let us consider this ladder of love, along each of the parts of the human being. It is a ladder that we can climb, level after level, gradually, and the higher we climb, the less important the physical aspect becomes. They do of course interpenetrate. So, let us look now in detail at each of the seven levels:

The love between man and woman at the level of the physical body is concerned with warmth. It's a matter of creating warmth—physical warmth—but also through caressing, kissing, sharing, holding the other in one's arms, the union.

At the etheric level, we are dealing with affection: tenderness, caring for, the gesture of kindness and attention toward the other (a flower, a poem, a phone call, and so on). It's the little surprise, the attention that one shows—the dialogue, and the communication between the two.

At the astral level, love bears the characteristic of desire: the longing, the thirst for the other—of his or her presence, voice. It's, of course, the closeness, the realm of sexual desire—at times, transcended, spiritualized. The harmonious interchange. It's also the emotion that brings the vision of the other, his or her personality: the smile, the charm, the beauty, the delight.

When we come to the I AM, we are dealing with recognition. It's the respect for the other, the acceptance of who he or she really is. It's the right to be different, the tolerance. It is to accept more faults and the lesser qualities in the other. It is the trust and the confidence that one has in the other person, the sincerity and the truth. It is, of course, the right to freedom of choice and movement. This is the sphere of recognition. I have recognized the beloved for what she truly is in her eternal nature. We have a glimpsed the true being of the other.

I would like to take these four first, before we go on to the higher members, because we meet not only positive qualities, but also the negatives ones.

So, if the love between man and woman is not harmonious, then at the physical level instead of bringing about love and warmth, it can chill the relationship, it becomes cold, frigid.

Affection, which is at the level of the etheric, turns into a lack of interest in the other and finally into indifference. The two partners have no further use for one another and start going their separate ways.

The realm of desire, which is the realm of passion, also has its negative aspect, where, for instance, each partner is only concerned with his or her own satisfaction, his or her own gratification, rather than feeling that in a relationship we want to satisfy what lives in the other person as desire, and not just seek our own gratification. Ultimately it will turn into repulsion, and rejection.

The sphere of the I AM, of recognition, is one that we can only understand if we think of the human being as consisting of a lower self and a higher self. What is the higher self? That is the eternal entity that lives within each one of us. What is the lower self? It is the persona, the personality. The word comes from the Latin which means "to sound through." Persona is the mask, through which one sounds.

When we meet one another, we meet, to begin with, the personality, which can be subject to shortcomings and unpleasant characteristics. It's the shadow side, in a way, of our being. But, within us there lives also the higher self. I would venture to say that when two people fall in love—one should reword it and say they *rise in love,* because they see in one another something of the eternal. This eternal element is quickening, it is the recognition: "I know you, and you know me!" Not only the physical, etheric, astral sheaths but something of that eternal self is recognized and also feels recognized in an harmonious relationship. That is a time when the sun shines strongly.

Sometimes it's called "the honeymoon," but one can also say that it's the sun shining clearly over both partners. There can also be moments when the sun is hidden behind the clouds and one doesn't see the higher self anymore because of the chores and the responsibilities of everyday life. That is why I think that in love that is harmonious, one would find that, at the level of the I AM, there is a recognition. When that ceases, then the opposite comes about. We don't see one another as clearly anymore and we also lose a certain amount of enthusiasm in the relationship. A feeling of being a stranger, of alienation prevails.

Those can be looked upon as four different levels of a ladder that can constantly be enhanced, worked over, and refined. Although the love relationship might start much more in the sexual-physical sphere and even a certain amount of lust being involved, it can be lifted into nobler aspects, depending of course on how the partners shape their lives.

Now, let us consider the three higher levels of the human being. Early on, I think, we spoke of the fact that in the life of the man, in the life of the woman, each seeks the complement of himself or herself and one can really come to the experience of: Yes, my life as a man is one-sided, just as the life of a woman is, and we really need one another in order to come to a certain completeness, to a certain fulfilment of our being. It is interesting to observe that when a couple meets and decides to be together and then travels, for example, to places where neither of the partners has been before, something further can happen. One discovers things together that one would not have discovered alone. That is the character of love at the level of the Spirit Self, of the Manas, which is revelation. Something is revealed to us, when we travel to Greece, to Egypt, to Mexico. We hasn't been there before, in this incarnation at least, and now in the course of our travels certain things come to our attention and this is like a revelation of something that concerns both of us and enhances the relationship.

When we think of love at the level of Buddhi, which is Life Spirit, we have yet another aspect—that love can be a healing, if one finds the right partner. Very often illnesses, a spiritual-soul illness of the past—in the form of disappointments, trials and ordeals—can find a healing because the beloved is there, and vice versa, of course. We are here for the other person, so there can be a real sense of healing, which one can understand also in connection with Buddha. The word Buddhi, of course, is related to Buddha, the master of compassion. Compassion contains healing; compassion is something that can bring about a new form of harmony.

When we speak of love at the level of Atman, which is Spirit Man, we are in a certain sense in the realm to which no human being has yet been able to rise. The only one in the whole development of humanity, so far, who has been able to develop love at the level of Atman is the Christ himself, who loves every single human being. Whether he or she is aware of the Christ or not is immaterial. The Christ as the cosmic being is the being of love, and his love is complete and has no conditions—is total unconditional love.

Unconditional love at that level can be translated as sacrifice. It is that particular reflection that we find in our human relationships when man and woman are able—are striving—to sacrifice for the sake of the other. It is like an offering, it need not be a burden, it need not constrain, it is rather a free gift of one's own soul-spiritual being for the other—simply because one has come to understand, to perceive, to love the other for what he or she is. I think that is where the two commandments of the Christ really begin to be meaningful. "Loving God with all one's heart" and "learning to love one's neighbor as oneself": those are the two commandments of love that the Christ brings us, as opposed to the ten commandments of Moses, which were largely concerned with what we should not do.

One can understand too, that in the age of Moses and beyond, it was a question of adhering to particular commandments because humanity was not ready yet for the freedom that came as a result of the Christ impulse. We should try to understand that the Christ brought freedom, and out of freedom love can blossom. If we are not free we cannot love, because then there would be constraint. Although many couples go through that lack of freedom and still try to find love, it is not really possible. Leaving the other person free means also to have absolute confidence and trust in the other person.

So, love grows out of the seedbed of freedom. It is interesting how Goethe put it; he was very perceptive in these matters and he said: "Love does not constrain; love forms, it fashions." If we think for a moment—if there is any constraint, fundamentally the love is not yet complete, the love is not yet perfect. We can be involved in a process, in a gradual process of transformation, but when love does not constrain then it can form, it can fashion. The picture that Goethe uses is "forming, fashioning," more or less in a way that the sculptor uses the clay to form the figure that he wishes to represent. The same forming and fashioning goes on when the couple lives together for a number of years and struggles, perhaps, to leave the other truly free.

I think we should try to understand these different levels not as fixed, but more as they flow one into the other. There are times when our love is more complete, more perfect, and at other times—just as there are days when one doesn't see the sun and the clouds restrict our view of the sunshine—we are thrown back on the dismal situation like what the weather might have created by way of rain, a certain sadness in the atmosphere. The important thing is to remind ourselves, again and again, and experience it in our hearts, that we have the possibility of transformation. "I am constantly attempting to love better." It is a process, not a finished, final condition. [See additional insights on the ladder of love in the Appendix.]

Q: *Can you speak of the destructive influence that Lucifer and Ahriman are providing in each of the spheres, given that Ahriman tries to separate people and Lucifer tries to take people away from the earth?*

A: The matter of the intervention of Lucifer and Ahriman is a very profound and subtle one. We should remember that within a female body, a person is much more open to a luciferic temptation. As we saw earlier on, a woman is not as deeply incarnated—although she gives birth to a child, she doesn't fall so heavily into the physical. Lucifer essentially attacks the astral body through emotionalism and so on, so if the relationship is not harmonious then Lucifer has already his influence in removing the person concerned from the middle ground.

On the other hand, men are more affected by the ahrimanic temptation. In other words, technology and the sciences fascinate men more than they do women. Ahriman is telling us all the time, "There is no such thing as spirituality, the spirit doesn't really exist," whereas a woman feels very deeply the existence of the spirit, she senses it. She may nevertheless fall into a situation where her relationship to the spirit can become excessive, especially through unbridled emotions.

The interesting thing is that in a harmonious relationship, a woman is the healing for a man and a man is the healing for a woman. Together they can also help one another to avoid extremes, and something of the Christ impulse begins to be born as a result of their being together. Where two or three—in this case two—are together in his name, the Christ can be there. The Christ can act, providing that, again, we are conscious of the fact that we can go to extremes, and that we should try always to find the middle ground, the golden mean.

Q: *If we are made in the image of God, why do we have physical needs, desires, sexual impulses?*

A: I think that to understand this, we have to go all the way back to the Paradise story. At one time, and this is beautifully illustrated—portrayed—in the Old Testament, in the first book of Moses, in Genesis, where we have the story of man and woman living in Paradise and eating of the Tree of Life and having been told by the Father God that they must not eat the fruit of the Tree of Knowledge of Good and Evil. We remember that in this idyllic situation, Lucifer appears and tempts the feminine part of our nature. That is the temptation through Eve. She receives an apple from the Tree of Knowledge of Good and Evil and bites into it and passes it to Adam and he ate. As a result, both fall, which means that they are expelled from Paradise and the Lord God says that from this moment onwards they are no longer allowed to eat from the Tree of Life. In the process of becoming conscious of the Tree of Knowledge of Good and Evil, we have lost the Paradise condition, we have come down on earth.

There are also three consequences as the result of our having been expelled, of having had to leave Paradise. On the one hand we have to work—*arbeit, travail,* work (we could go into the details regarding the origin of these words). Everyone on earth has to work in whatever form; that is a karmic situation. We all have to learn to suffer. Women particularly have to suffer through their periods, which start around the age of twelve or thirteen, and shed blood. And of course also, in the travail, in the pain of giving birth to children. The whole question of suffering comes now into the picture, and the third aspect is death. Death is part of life. One might say, from that moment that we are born, we are destined to die. From the moment of our birth, we go toward death. If we consider these three aspects, we find too that as a result of having eaten of the Tree of Knowledge of Good and Evil, we have become aware of our nakedness; we have fallen into the physical body. The I AM, as such, in its divine origin, activated the physical body from outside, but now we are dwelling in the physical. From now onwards, the act of procreation begins to take place more consciously between man and woman.

This whole question of sexuality is of course connected with creativity. What is interesting is that the Bible says: And Adam knew his wife. What does that mean? It means that Adam had sexual intercourse with his wife Eve. Knowledge, knowing can be either through sexuality (man and woman coming together in that sphere) or we can also know in a different way, in a soul-spiritual sense. These two forms of knowing are related. We have the upper aspect of knowledge, our thinking capacities and so on, and we have the other aspect of creation, of procreation, that has to do with sexuality. That is of course a great mystery. In our language we have that we conceive of an idea, but we also conceive a child—two different forms of conception—one in the realm of thought and one in the realm of sexuality.

Now, because of the luciferic temptation, sex can be practiced without love. That is perfectly possible, but it also debases it, it also drags it down. Although Lucifer incites it, Ahriman really draws us, then, into a sphere that can be dangerous, indeed—in which a man will just pursue a woman, not because he has any affection or warmth for her as an individual, but simply in order to gratify his own sexual instincts—the Don Juan type of situation. Fundamentally, we have man, the male part of the human being that can be also the corrupter of woman and the woman who can also exercise her "Lilith power." (You will remember that Lilith was the other wife of Adam—that he had two wives.) Eve was the true one, you might say, and Lilith was the temptress. The Lilith part of a woman can draw man away from his better self and corrupt him. Corruption is possible on both sides; here the interventions of Lucifer and Ahriman play a part when a lack of harmony prevails.

Q: *You mentioned "when two are gathered in my name." What if two men, or two women come together? Does that present some problems?*

A: I think that we are entering in a sphere that is extremely difficult. Why is it so difficult? Because in homosexuality or lesbianism we have something that is like an exceptional situation in relation to sexuality. One has then to understand whether that is wholesome and healthy, harmonious, or not. And why is this taking place more and more? Perhaps it is because there is so little understanding between the sexes—that some men prefer to associate with other men rather than to *face the challenge* of what a woman represents and equally when women come together in preference to having a relationship with a man because *they don't want to take up that challenge either*. It may be part of our civilization's problem, where there is so little understanding and in common parlance that we are witnessing this "war of the sexes." If that is true, little harmony can be found. As I mentioned earlier, one ought to replace it by saying we are striving—one should or can be striving—for "the peace of the sexes." If that takes place, I think that many aspects of homosexuality would disappear.

Third Interview
November 22, 1996
Fair Oaks, California

Q: *Could you please speak of the differences and similarities in the four elements that compose the human being. In the light of the differences, how should man and woman interact with each other?*

A: We have already seen on a previous occasion that man and woman are different, and each represents one aspect of the total image of the human being. If we consider that for a moment, there will be a predominance of certain members in man and a different predominance of members in a woman. Of course, that doesn't mean that any of the two doesn't have all of the four elements, but again, we are speaking of *predominances.*

I AM (EGO)	Man
ASTRAL	Woman
ETHERIC	Woman
PHYSICAL	Man

You might say that in a woman what predominates is the astral and the etheric element. We can understand that quite easily because it is only through a woman that a child can be born and she needs the life forces in order to give birth to the child and also to be able to carry that child within her uterus for ten lunar months. We can also understand why the astral body predominates, because a woman is deeply connected with her feelings, with her emotions, and in a rather different way than a man is. Now, in a male incarnation, what predominates is the I AM, and its relationship with the physical, so that there is something like a short circuit between the I AM and the physical. Although he, too, has an astral and etheric body, they do not play an equal part—but that enables man to be more active outwardly and the woman to be more sensitive inwardly. If we consider an harmonious working between the sexes, then the feeling is that they will be complementing each other, and we might be arriving at something more fully human than if they were separate.

Q: *You just mentioned that there is a sort of short circuit in man, between his I AM and his physical—what did you mean by that?*

A: Well, the danger is that men are not sufficiently in touch with their own feelings and so they act, they do things, but it doesn't affect their soul life as deeply. Until recently, it was thought to be totally unmasculine to cry, to weep. On the other hand women tend to have a particular weakness and that is over-emotionalism. Through a harmonious working between the two, man can find his own self more easily and the woman can become less emotional; they can balance a few things out, more harmoniously.

Q: *How can the man nourish the two elements in the woman and how can the woman nourish the two elements in the man?*

A: The man has to learn to be attentive to the needs of the woman. That can also mean to buy little things, like a box of chocolate, flowers—in other words, to give her something that shows appreciation and love, not to forget her birthday, or wedding anniversary and so on. To be caring in that sort of way, I think, is very important. Also, to be helpful in the house, to be of assistance in the household.

What a woman creates for a man is equally important, because she is the one really who makes the home; she is the homemaker. When we go to visit a couple in their house, we usually find that it is the woman who has created the surroundings, the way the furniture is arranged, the way the curtains are displayed, how the whole lay-out of the room is done and so on—and that is a particular caring.

A woman certainly if she loves her companion, will have affection for him, and will try to make his life as relaxing as possible, especially when he comes back after a day's work with all the worries and stresses and strain that that implies. I think that there is a great deal of room for mutual support and mutual help. Much will also depend on how we speak to one another. Do we take time to communicate in a warm, respectful, and understanding way—or is it all too much—and a cold silence reigns?

Q: *Can you tell us how society has evolved from matriarchy to patriarchy?*

A: It is not an easy matter. There have been in the past matriarchal societies where women were given the rulership of the family, or the clan, of the nation even. The Amazons, of course, are a case in point, out of Greek mythology and still to this day, that plays quite an important part. For example, someone told me that you can't really become an Israeli citizen unless you have Jewish blood on your mother's side; that is the determining factor. In the Arab world you have these extraordinary and strange separations between men and women, but the women—although they do not appear in public—still exert a considerable role in the family. The grandmother and the mother are looked upon with great respect and love. So, although the men are outwardly active, the women hold a central place in their communities.

Q: *What about the bible and the story of Abraham and the two women?*

A: Abraham had two sons. The first son of Abraham was Isaac and he represents the Hebrew stream. The second son was Ishmael who represents the Arab stream. Later on the two tribes separated and they became antagonistic.

Of course there are books that you can read yourself to find the women in the Bible and they are very important, but throughout the Old Testament you will find that it is the men who tend to be the active ones. It is Moses who takes his people across the desert for forty years, it is David who fights various battles in order to secure the kingdom and there are many other examples where the patriarchs and the important male figures of the Old Testament provide the lead in what happens in their countries and to their people. Yet the women in the background play, of course, an essential part; if you think of Ruth or Bathsheba, the wife of David, who gave birth to Solomon. There are always women, and they play a large part, but their role is not outwardly manifested to the same extent as a man's.

Q: *Can you speak of how the four elements—fire, water, air and earth—play into the temperament of man and woman, and particularly in their relationships?*

A: That is very difficult, because the temperament are not divided up into a particular gender, but each human being has his or her own temperament and one can't say that women are more sanguine and that men are more melancholic; I don't think this is quite valid. It is a matter of the individual, because we are talking about the constitution of the ether body, the life forces that are divided onto four components (the four elements). These life forces are more attracted to one or another element depending on the nature of the incarnation. Those more attracted to the fire might have a choleric temperament. Attraction to air would make one more sanguine—to earth would make one more melancholic, and to water more phlegmatic. The same is true for men and women. I really don't think that we can divide up those temperaments between male and female, that is much more individual to each person.

Q: *You don't feel that trying to create artificially a relationship out of matching two temperament, male and female would help very much?*

A: I don't think so.

Q: *What about the stability and conservatism of men versus women seeking always novelty and changes, saying, "Can we try this or that," instead of men being satisfied with what already exists, with the status quo?*

A: At this particular level, one would have to say that it is the woman who brings a certain amount of steadiness, through history as well, and it is the man who inserts new elements! That is one thing we should really observe. Inventors are usually men, innovators. It is not women; women are in that sense very conservative, out of their instinctual nature, that is true. Then you have the other aspect, women can be very light-hearted, very capricious. That is a certain sanguinity, you might say, though this is also a character trait. This "trying new things" in women is certainly true at a certain level. Equally men like to have a certain steadiness, which is so wonderful if they have a harmonious and comfortable home life. It steadies their impetuous nature—they are always wanting to do something! We have to consider that men actually change history. Yes, women are the builders, the ones who protect, the ones who give also warmth to situations but men are prepared to branch out—and also leave a woman behind in order to branch out! For example, take a job where the man is away most of the week and can only come home on week-ends. A woman, given the choice, wouldn't do that because she has her home, she has her children—by nature she wouldn't do that.

Q: *You spoke earlier of the tendency of men to move always towards the ideal in womanhood and to seek many relationships in the process . . .?*

A: Well you see, in falling in love, which I like to call "rising in love," a woman discovers the higher self of a man, and she is not so inclined, after she has found this man, to look around for other opportunities. That is so if the man is worthy of respect, is striving, does things around the house, and so on. By and large, once she has found the man she deeply feels connected with, she will be faithful, she will want to remain with him. But a woman can also be disillusionned. Men are differently constituted and they are always looking for an ideal and they might not have found it, or they might have found it partially in their wife. So, what happens is that they start looking somewhere else! Is there perhaps someone else who represents this ideal of the eternal feminine more completely than the woman I am with? It is, of course, the Don Juan tendency and that causes endless problems. The woman has been seduced, and feels that she gave herself to that man in good faith, out of confidence, and then, if the man turns and goes away, the pain she feels gnaws on her organism. It is not just the pain of the separation, it goes right down into her organism, into her etheric and astral—particularly into her etheric body. Her life forces have been attacked by this situation. A relationship goes more deeply in a woman generally because it does not only affect her feelings but also her organism. But a man is not like that at all. In case of a separation, he goes on!—finds perhaps solace, comforts himself in his work, until he has found some other partner. A woman finds that much more difficult, because it enters so deeply into her organism as a result of the sexual relationship in which she was involved.

Q: *So, there is definitely a step between "encountering" somebody and having sexual intercourse? What is really affected—the etheric?*

A: Oh yes, definitely! I think that in meeting a woman that one likes and respects, it can become a friendship, it can become the level of *philia,* that we spoke of earlier. If too quickly it falls into sexuality, into eroticism, and if that eroticism is not going to be steady, is not going to be something for the future, then it will hurt the woman more than it is going to hurt the man. Often men don't realize sufficiently what they are doing to women. It is not just a saying that a woman is "heart broken," it is literally true, because it affects her life process so deeply. One should know that when one enters too quickly into a relationship without knowing that it is going to have a future, suffering is going to ensue. It is interesting to note that in French and also in English, we have the word passion, which can mean two things: the passion in a relationship, in other words of a sexual nature, and we also speak of the Passion of Christ, when we speak of the suffering of Christ, and it is the same word. We have another component in compassion. What does it really mean? It means "to suffer with." You are a compassionate human being if you can suffer with another, so that his or her suffering becomes your suffering. In German it's *Mitleid; Leid* means to suffer and *Mit* means with. To suffer with, that is what compassion is and we have to learn to develop that capacity.

Q: *It's not only pleasure.*

A: Not at all!

Q: *Why do some people have a marriage that lasts forty years, and why do some others, men or women, have four, five, six meaningful relationships in their life?*

A: That is of course a karmic matter. One can't judge that. In our time, a number of incarnations from the past focus and come together in one. So maybe you might have a relationship of one time, ancient Egypt, but later on in this life, you might have a relationship that comes over from Greece, or a third relationship that comes over from the Middle Ages and they all telescope in a short time.

Q: *Can they choose a schedule, to present themselves over many incarnations?*

A: No, not necessarily, because this is a particular incarnation in which a lot of things have to come together and sort themselves out for the future, in order not to be burdened by all sorts of constraints. One can notice that the older one gets, if we look back to the first twenty-five years of our life, and think of ourself now and we think of ourself in the past, it is as if we are two different people. We can hardly recognize ourselves. How different we are from twenty-five to fifty; it's another whole life time! If you look back in your seventies or so to when you were fifty, it' s a whole different story again. It's a different aspect, it's like three lives in one!

Q: *Do we meet only people that help us to progress?*

A: No, no. I mean there are all sorts of temptations!—because Lucifer and Ahriman are always trying to intervene, to interfere with the normal, harmonious, healthy development of the human being. Lucifer comes in particularly in the younger years, with too much euphoria perhaps, with tremendous enthusiasm, that it can be overdone—with pride—with the feeling that one is "on top of the world." After thirty-five it's the Ahrimanic that comes in as a temptation, a hardening process, a lack of flexibility.

Q: *Does this hardening affect our relationships?*

A: Oh very much. Because for a relationship to remain young—not in years necessarily but in spirit—there has to be a certain flexibility, a willingness to learn from the other, at any time. When we are young, we are adjusting, but when people marry later on, both partners have their set ways. If they marry at thirty-five or forty and are prepared to be flexible, it might yield a harmonious relationship.

Q: *How much should one give of himself or herself to a relationship, whether we are married or not?*

A: That, you can't say. The best thing would be to give all. But some people can't do that; it depends on the individual concerned. Now, I was reading in the newspaper that many people who get married today have prenuptial agreements. The moment they are in love, they want to get married but it might not last. . . . The woman has a firm and is an executive, and she wants a prenuptial agreement, so that if her husband wants to divorce her, he will not be able to run away with the firm or vice versa. Heartfelt confidence is in short supply.

Q: *Can you speak of the double and the role it plays in relationships.?*

A: We have spoken previously of the different levels of love in the case of a certain harmony, when there is genuine warmth and affection and desire in the sexual sphere is fulfilling. There is recognition and revelation, and healing, and a sense of sacrifice in the relationship (I refer to the sketch of the seven levels of Love). On the other side, we have to put what is the result of the double—or if you like, when the love relationship is no longer harmonious—then we find that the negative aspects, both in men and women, rear up against one another, and we have the situation of *Who's Afraid of Virginia Woolf.* Two stars who have been in the limelight for many years in that connection are Elizabeth Taylor and Richard Burton. If we think of them—Richard Burton of course has died, but if we think of their Golden years—they had positive and wonderful years. Then they turned against one another; that is not the better part of themselves, but it is the lower part of themselves. We all have that, we all have a double. Goethe speaks of two souls that live in his breast. A soul that strives upwards, and another that is chained to the earthly things.

In the working of the double, we have something very destructive, very wounding, ruthless. And just in relationships, that double can be brought out quickly, if the two parties are not aware of what is happening to themselves, because the negative, the warring condition between the partners, the misunderstandings, the nasty words, are of course, inspired by Lucifer and Ahriman. They use, they fire the life of the double, they nourish it.

At the physical level, instead of having warmth, we have cold—a cold relationship. Instead of tenderness and affection, we have, in the etheric sphere, indifference.

At the level of the astral—of the desire sphere—instead of having a harmonious interchange at the level of the soul and sexuality, hate enters, self gratification.

Instead of the recognition into the sphere of the I AM, we suddenly fail to see the other person at all, or rather, choose to see only their negative side, when we previously saw something of their true self, of their true higher-self. There is no more revelation and life together becomes dull. We can see that often, in middle aged couples when they travel, how nothing very much happens to bring a new element. So, instead of a relationship being healing, it becomes the opposite. It becomes an illness, a disease, and makes both partners sick. We can see that easily if we stay too long in a relationship that is not harmonious, and which turns in the direction where it's better for the two to separate, because the actual health of each partner is being attacked. It may be the physical health, but it can affect also the soul health; there is absolute dismay, there is a feeling of lack of balance.

At the level of Atman, we can see clearly that we are not yet able, in a positive sense, to be as sacrificial, perhaps, as we should be. And the negative side is utter egoism. Wanting things in a relationship simply for oneself, not being prepared to give of oneself for the other.

Q: *You used many times the word harmonious; what do you mean by harmonious in the couple? What represents harmony and how important is it?*

A: Harmony: one can use a musical analogy. There are pieces of music that are harmonious and then there are those that are discordant. And the discord arises when notes of music come together and they don't really meet properly. Harmony is the musical word, but I think it's a good one, because there could be harmony at different levels. It can be harmonious in the sphere of sexuality, it can be harmonious in the soul sphere—we share the same ideas, we are of the same mind, we are striving for the same things, etc. There can be harmony on the level of the spirit, it confirms that we are on the same spiritual path.

Q: *How?*

A: That our ideas of life after death, of life before birth, our ideas of sleep, and what sleep is, that these things begin to shine in a spiritual truth that we both share. It is not one partner who has these intuitions. It can also become a study for some time, where for example you feel that you want to read the John Gospel together. That is much more of the nature of *agape,* it is much more of a nature of spiritual love. There is an expression in French: *Les grands esprits finissent toujours par se rencontrer.* (Great minds sooner or later always meet.)

Q: *Do chance meetings occur?*

A: I don't think so. In other words, when we say "It happened by coincidence—it was a chance meeting;" then we have not understood what lies behind that meeting. Because every meeting with another person is there for a specific purpose. The purpose can be looked at in different ways: one, we can learn something from every person—from a child, from an old man, from a simple peasant woman—it doesn't matter. They do not have to be intelligent, but it is simply one person meeting another, heart to heart. Every person has something to teach us, and we hope that we, in turn, can bring something to the other person, that is, a particular way of thinking. That is thinking along karmic lines. Where do these meetings come from? They come from the past. I am meeting someone now for the first time in this incarnation because of the past. But I meet them by going towards them and they are going towards me, so my past lies in my future; that's the paradox! There was a time when we had not met yet, right? I didn't know that you existed then, and you didn't know me either. Well, you may have known my name. Then one meets—the meeting happens—and afterward it has certain repercussions, certain influences, as a shaping of the destiny of the two people or more that meet and exchange and so on. We have either a recognition straight away, and it can happen that one falls in love, for example "at first sight," but it can also happen that we meet a person of the opposite sex, and it might take us five years before we "see" them—because, we see them, like anybody else, but suddenly we discover "something," and that is a very important moment! What is it that we discover that we haven't seen before? What I think that we discover is a spark of the divine, of the higher self in the other person. Love has to do with the recognition of the essential, of the humanity in the other, and that is beyond the physical, etheric, astral; it concerns the eternal self, the I AM.

Now, it is interesting that we say about chance meetings: it was a coincidence that we happened to meet—but I like to say that it's a veil. A friend of mine in France who is Jewish told me once, when I spoke of *par hasard* (which in English means "by chance"—it has really nothing to do with "hasard" as in the English word), and I said "well, I know only the old meaning which is 'by coincidence,' 'by chance,' and he said, "If you go back to the Hebrew roots of the word, of these two words, it actually means 'as God wills it.'"So, we can have the most extraordinary feeling about this. The meeting was "as God willed it." God willed it—I didn't; you didn't! It's a wonderful thought. It was intended to happen in our destinies.

Q: *Some people feel that if you meet someone sexually, that there is nothing wrong with it; that is sufficient, that is enough.*

A: Well, that depends of course on your way of life. It's enough only at one stage. Usually, if it happens very quickly, it is something that is not going to be lasting.

Q: *Is that necessarily a negative experience—one that stays on the physical level?*

A: The point is, of course, how sensitive the people are. If you go from one partner to the other, and you do not suffer from the separation, from the severance, then there is a certain insensitivity. Many young people today indulge in sex without love being involved. This can be harmful, and encourages promiscuity. But we can also learn to become more sensitive. We might make mistakes in that sphere as young people. These things come about and then we might say: wait a moment, I can't go on living like this! One could add: I can't go on living like this from one woman/man to the other, because it is too painful. It is too painful because we invest something when we unite with another person, and when that is taken away it is painful, so it depends on our sensitivity. But one can't generalize; every instance is unique. Not so long ago, there was the meeting, and then after a certain time, you had an engagement, then a year or two after, you had a marriage.... My Goodness, everything was very, very slow.

Q: *And rhythmical?*

A: And rhythmical—but now we live in very, very fast times. People might feel that they might lose it if they don't do it quickly. They'll say: I might lose you!

Q: *Where does this "I might lose you"—that insecurity—come from?*

A: Yes, that is also a lack of confidence in karma. If you are meant to be together, it will work out. That is the extraordinary thing!

Q: *Despite all obstacles and everybody?*

A: Yes, if it is meant to be, it will work out! . . . .

Q: *By "meant to be," do you mean on a long term basis?*

A: Yes, for example. Or for a longer term.

Part Two
Essays

Introduction

It is with awareness of great hazards that I venture to write about the mystery of love in our time. The topic is rife with misunderstandings. The very word "love" varies wildly in meaning according to the way it is used. I *love* oranges, my Volvo, a Bruckner symphony, my family. Though we use the same word to indicate our feelings about many things, the quality of our connections differs vastly. When we ponder the quality of a mother's love for her children, or a husband's for his wife, or a human being's for his God, it is as if we lift veil after veil, as if we enter a mystery.

The root of "mystery" is the Greek word *mystos*, which means "keeping silence." Webster's Ninth New Collegiate Dictionary tells us that the word "mystery" means "a religious truth that one can know only by revelation and cannot fully understand." So, a being of truth who keeps silent lives near to love. It is this being of truth toward whom we are drawn in the reflection on the mystery of love.

When we look into contemporary culture, we might see with dismay a tendency to devalue anything of a sacred or noble aspect in the relationship of man and woman. People speak glibly of the war of the sexes. Why war? Where is the harmony, the fulfillment, of the union of man and woman? Cynicism has become an all too familiar companion to men and women seeking relationships today. "Can I really trust him?" she says suspiciously. "What does she really want?" he says doubting. Others cast suspicions and doubts aside and plunge into intimate relations from the start; cynicism too often follows later. Can two people build a life together upon the flower-petal fragility of an emotion called love, or start a family because the sex-called-love is good? Millions wonder if they will ever find their way to a lasting, loving relationship.

No, love is not clear to us. But why would it be so, when the nature of being human is not so very clear. Is the human being an animal? Thirty years ago Desmond Morris's *Man, the Naked Ape* caused a stir, but why, when Darwin (1809–1882) and Haeckel (1834–1919) had long provided us with the picture of man as descended from the animals. It is insidious, for if, indeed, we are no better than naked apes, it is not surprising that we would behave increasingly like animals—and especially in the realm of the instinctive functions of mating and sexuality. Animals can only love—if we can use that term—in relationship to their instinctual nature, but human beings are capable of more.

Many people today regard the human being more as some sort of machine. This idea is not new, either. It was introduced by Julien Offray de Lamettrie (1707–1751), a physician and philosopher, who wrote a number of popular books, including *L'Homme machine* (Man the machine) and *L'Art de jouir* (The art of enjoyment) in which the only virtue is that of the senses and the development of self-love. Death marks the end of a farce, according to Lamettrie. Life's all a game.

French philosopher Blaise Pascal (1623–1662) expressed it succinctly when he said: *L'homme n'est ni ange, ni bête, mais qui veut faire l'ange fait souvent la bête.* He makes a play on words here that is not easily translated, but we might say, "Man is neither angel nor beast, and he who constantly thinks that he is an angel makes a fool of himself, makes a beast of himself." We are poised between the angelic and the animalistic. We share in both worlds. And what I observe being obscured in modern consciousness is the angelic part of our being. I might call this angelic part, which we all share and which strives beyond the merely instinctual, all the qualities of soul and spirit that lift us above the animal, that give us the individual life a machine could never have.

Views of man as animal, man as machine underlie the teachings we give our children today about love. Learn about the mechanics of your body and learn about the techniques of relating to others. How often do we teach them about romance, how one soul meets another, the art of loving? Are teens today taken through the great love stories through the ages? Are they taught to appreciate the intimate soul union of a Romeo and Juliet against all the odds of warring families, or of the faithfulness of a Penelope as she waits for the return of husband Odysseus from the Trojan War and their eventual reunion after twenty years? Do they hear the sonnets of Shakespeare? Do they learn to respond to the ideals expressed by the Romantic poets? Who today has read the beautiful description of love found in Plato's Symposium? There, love is discussed from various points of view and crowned by Socrates' views of love, learned from Diotima, a wise woman, who has insight into the noble, spiritually enriching ideal nature of love.

My observation is that the sexual revolution has largely ruled out these considerations. We think we are too smart for ideals. We smirk at those who hold them. We prefer "reality." Forsaking the idea, we give instead practical instruction to youngsters so that they can avoid the quicksand and aberrations of sexual intercourse. Values are overlooked while safe sex is emphasized without connecting it with the nobler aspects of love.The sexual revolution of the 1960s is sometimies considered a freeing, a liberation from the tight Victorian traditions—but license and promiscuity in the sexual field is not true freedom. Freedom rightly undertood always implies responsibillity.

In an age of increasing individualism, sexuality without love becomes an anonymous activity, whereas in a destiny connection between a man and woman, love is always unique and individual.

We shall examine more closely what is meant by "falling in love." The realization brings wonder and joy. We see the other, we behold something more in the other than simply the physical. While by no means excluding the attraction we feel, we behold something of the eternal in the other, as well. This experience quickens a deep inner conviction that this is the person whom we love and wish to cherish. It may happen at first sight or after a long time when we have come to know one another and a veil falls from our eyes. We experience the beloved in a comprehensive way, with the gaze of the soul as well as with physical eyes.

Perhaps falling in love should be renamed "rising in love."

That sexual attraction may play a powerful part is undeniable and wholesome, but the soul-spiritual aspects are equally important and will shape the relationship as it develops over the weeks, the months, and the years. We can, then, begin to ask ourselves, Why have we met? Is it mere coincidence? Is the fact that the loved one enters our life a mere accident? Is not something of a mystery involved in our being brought together? Poets during the past two hundred years have expressed the wonder of this mystery.

This motif is treated intimately and sensitively in the famous poem by Johann Wolfgang von Goethe (1749–1832), "Why did you give us the deep glances?" which Goethe wrote to Charlotte Von Stein (1742–1827) in April 1776 when he arrived in Weimar in Germany at the age of twenty-six. Feeling that their friendship was rooted in a distant past, he wrote:

> Tell me, what does destiny hold in store for us?
> Tell me, what bound us together so perfectly?
> Oh, in time long past,
> You were my sister or my wife.

Goethe wrote these lines the evening after he first met Charlotte. She was seven years his senior, a married woman with children. This relationship would affect Goethe's heart and mind for the next twenty years. Their lives were deeply shaped by this recognition, which was mutual.

Goethe's words are not poetic metaphor; they are to be taken literally. We find proof of this in a letter to Christoph-Martin Wieland (1733–1813) that Goethe wrote to his friend in the same month:

> I can explain the significance, the power which this woman has over me, in no other way than through the transmigration of souls—yes, we were once man and wife—now we know of each other—in a veiled way, in a spiritual atmosphere—I have no name for us—the past—the future—the old.

And in a letter written to Charlotte some years later, Goethe states his belief in reincarnation in unambiguous terms:

> I long to leave this place. The spirits of time gone by allow me not one happy hour here. I've not wanted to climb a single mountain; everything remains soiled by unpleasant memories. How good it is that man dies in order to extinguish the memories and plans to return again.

The same thought is expressed somewhat differently in a grand image in Goethe's "Song of the Spirits over the Waters":

> The soul of Man
> Resembleth the water.
> From heaven it cometh
> To heaven it soareth
> And then again
> To earth descendeth
> Changing ever.

For Goethe it became apparent that the entelechy, the I AM, in every human being, is subject to reincarnation. The body provides an instrument for the spirit, but this instrument is temporal, subject to birth and death. The I AM is the eternal part in each of us.

If we seriously consider the idea of karma and reincarnation, a view of love and of the relationship between man and woman might be immeasurably enhanced and deepened.

The first of these essays deal with an historical aspect and an overview of love through the ages, from Plato to Solovyiev. We shall approach this theme in the works of Dante, Shakespeare, Goethe, Novalis and Solovyiev. These represent highlights in Western civilization, and, of course, are not exhaustive.

In the second part of this book, an attempt will be made to discuss contemporary questions leading to the ideal of love, *agape*, in the John Gospel and Saint Paul's letter to the Corinthians. A chapter is also devoted to the views of Rudolf Steiner (1861–1925), which contain a totally novel way of considering the Mystery of Love. The last chapter is devoted to examples of sacred and profane love in paintings by Titian and Rembrandt, as well as the portraits of Christ by Leonardo da Vinci and Rembrandt.

I met the work of Rudolf Steiner more than fifty years ago when I was twenty-one, and, ever since, his impulse has been a major force in my life. I wish to acknowledge that I could not have written these essays without his all-encompassing inspiration. His insights into the reality of reincarnation and karma have been invaluable.

1

Love Among the Greeks

Love makes the world go round. Love makes life possible. In other words, without attraction between men and women, without the sexual union that follows, and without the loving willingness to give birth to a baby and raise it, the human race could not continue. With this constant, however, our attitudes towards love and relationships have changed considerably over the years.

The further back we trace in history, the more we find that marriages were arranged without much regard for the individuals involved. Whether or not the young man and young woman felt love toward one another was of little importance in arranged marriages. What mattered was that one stayed within the bloodline, kept within the tribe, married into the right family with the social advantage that such a union might create. Emancipation from family tradition and convention emerged within the last five hundred years and reflects individualization, which is part of a new consciousness of humanity. Today, marriages across religious lines and racial boundaries still may stir hatred in some, unease in others, but they are increasingly gaining acceptance. The family continues to play a role in one's relationship with others, but in the western world, young people seek at an early age to go their own way and find the partner of their choice.

If we glance toward ancient Greece, we find that during the Golden Age of the great philosophers, the belief was alive that love was a spiritual being. The Greeks named him Eros, the Romans Cupid. He is often represented as a baby or a small child, to characterize love's purity and innocence. The mischievous Cupid, with whom we may be more familiar than with Eros, was preceded by a powerful being whose divine status was recognized. She was called Aphrodite by the Greeks and Venus by the Romans. She wove between human beings, enkindling feelings of attraction that would result in union within the earthly realm. Her son was called Love.

In Plato's Symposium we find a wonderful discussion of this deity called Love. Socrates has invited a number of guests for a meal, and one after another around the table each presents his view of Love. When Socrates takes his turn, he prefers not to speak his own thoughts but reports those he has heard from Diotima, a wise woman who speaks out of the authority of the Mysteries.

Diotima: Love is halfway between mortal and immortal. He is a Great Spirit.

Socrates. Everything that is of the nature of the spirit is half God and half Man. And what is the function of such a being?

Diotima: To interpret and convey messages to the gods from humans, and to humans from the gods, prayers and sacrifices from the one and commands and rewards from the other. Being of an intermediate nature, a spirit bridges the gap between them, and prevents the universe from falling into two separate halves. Through this class of beings come all divination, and the supernatural skills of priests in sacrifice and rights and spells and every kind of magic and wizardry. The gods don't deal directly with the human being. It is by means of the spirits that all the intercourse and communication of gods with humans, both in waking life and in sleep, is carried on. A man who possesses skill in such a matter is a spiritual man, whereas a man whose skill is confined to trade or handicraft is an earthly creature. Spirits are many in number and of many kinds, and one of them is Love.

The conversation then leads to Love's parentage. He is a son of Aphrodite. Shortly after this interchange, an important matter is introduced by Diotima—the concept of change:

> A man, for example, is called the same name from boyhood to old age. He does not in fact

> retain the same attributes, although he is called the same person; he is always becoming a new being, and undergoing a process of loss and reparation, which affects his hair, his flesh, his bones, his blood, and his whole body. And not only his body, but his soul as well. No man's character, habits, opinions, desires, pleasures, pains, and fears remain always the same! New ones come into existence, and old ones disappear.

Socrates ends on a final note:

> This, Phaedrus and my other friends, is what Diotima said and what I believe. And because I believe it, I try to persuade that in the acquisition of this blessing, human nature can find no better helper than Love. I declare that it is the duty of every man to honor Love. And I honor and practice the mysteries of Love in a special degree myself and recommend the same to others. And I praise the power and valor of Love to the best of my ability, both now and always.

We can readily see that in this discussion among the early Greeks, love was regarded as both mortal and immortal, earthly and spiritual. Indeed, the Greeks distinguished three aspects or levels of Love: Eros, the love of the physical, which encompasses also tenderness, affection, and the caresses exchanged between the lovers. Then there is Philia, which is the love of the soul, a deep friendship, for instance; the feeling that one has met one's soulmate; a heartfelt sentiment. Finally, they recognized Agape, the stage that denotes the love of the spirit, spiritual love—the highest and most exalted form of the union between two human beings but also of man or woman with the divine. Whereas Eros belongs to the passing moment, Agape carries in it an element of the eternal.

The Greeks perceived the levels of love as like a ladder that leads from the intimacies of physical love to all the degrees of soul connection to a spiritual bond beyond the physical and bodily limitations. Is there an incompatibility between Eros and Agape? Between the earthly Aphrodite-Pandemos of Plato and his sublime Aphrodite-Urania? This will be examined later in the essay on the sevenfold ladder of love.

I need to add one footnote to this discussion of love among the Greeks. The common expression, "platonic love," is not found in the writings of Plato. As the term is used commonly today, it indicates a deep connection between two people that involves no sexuality of any sort. However, much to some people's surprise, the love to which Plato refers mostly includes sexuality. It is his emphasis on the pure, ideal element of love that distinguishes his discussion of it. What is meant today by platonic love might better be replaced with the term "Philia love"; in other words, a love of soul, interwoven with affection, that excludes the sexual. According to Plato, sexual love includes an ideal element.

2

Dante
From Earthly to Eternal Love

However sketchy one's survey of love and lovers throughout the ages might be, it becomes apparent that in the western world after the advent of Christ, love between man and woman becomes more individual, more personal. We can see the gradual emergence of the love that recognizes the individual in the works of Dante when he speaks of his beloved Beatrice. Admittedly, lovers were passionate for one another in western literature before the thirteenth century, so we may say that Dante, the great Italian poet, expresses for them all, in the most sublime manner, the particular feelings of the lover toward his beloved.

Dante Alighieri, born in Florence in 1265, belonged to a noble but impoverished family. At the age of nine he beheld Beatrice for the first time. She was eight years of age, a beautiful, radiant young girl. At first sight he fell deeply in love with her. Some eight years later he saw her again. She was now a grown young woman, beautiful beyond compare, gracious, enchanting, fascinating. His childhood infatuation was now kindled into a greater fire, which only a poet could express, and this is exactly what Dante began to do.

Over a period of several years he wrote *La Vita Nuova* (The new life), a series of sonnets and commentaries that express the sublimity of his feelings for Beatrice and how she gave him new life of soul. It appears that he tried to approach her directly, but she declined his attentions, much to his deep disappointment. She married another and died at the young age of twenty-four. The sonnets reveal his experiences with her in Florence and also tell us in a most intimate way of his supersensible experiences connected to her. He foresaw her death, and after her passing he had two visions of her, one in the purity of her childhood, the other of Beatrice among the angels. It is Beatrice, he writes, that leads him to a glimpse of the eternal feminine in the cosmos.

Dante's sonnets and their commentaries are unique in the history of literature. They express clearly, in a form for all to read, what the nature of sublime love can really be. The poetry is not affected; it comes from the heart and enters the heart of the reader. Dante completed the cycle of sonnets by the time he was thirty. His love of Beatrice and her great gift in leading him to the eternal feminine were to inspire the poet's writings for the next twenty-five years.

Around 1300, when Dante was thirty-five, having reached the mid-point of life, he writes of experiences at the threshold to the spiritual world with three beasts that appeared to attack him. These experiences mark the opening of the *La Divina Comedia,* a monumental poem. In it, he first speaks of Hell, which he traverses under the guidance of Virgil. Virgil (70–19 BC) was a poet who wrote the most influential work of Ancient Roman literature, the *Aeneid,* a mythological epic in twelve books describing the seven-year wanderings of Aeneas from the fall of Troy to his military victory in Italy. During the Middle Ages philosophical meanings were read into the *Aeneid,* and Virgil was considered a seer, prophet, and magician. Not only Dante Alighieri, but also Geoffrey Chaucer, Edmund Spenser, John Milton and Alfred Lord Tennyson claimed to be indebted to Virgil and his work.

Subsequently, Dante enters Purgatory, still led by Virgil, and toward the end of his journey there, we meet Beatrice, who becomes his spiritual guide through all the circles of Paradise. Only she, his beloved, who had died many years earlier, would now be able to guide him in the lofty regions of the universe—Beatrice, who represents for Dante the eternal feminine. She guides him through Paradise, a spiritual journey upward through the planets and the hierarchies. It is the journey of the soul after death.

In Canto XXXI of the *Paradiso,* Beatrice takes her leave, and Dante is, to begin with, startled by her departure.

> Without reply I looked up to that height
> And saw her draw an aureole round herself
> As she reflected the eternal light.

No mortal I though plunged to the last bounds
of the deeper sea has ever been so far
from the top most heaven to which the thunder sound

I was then from Beatrice, but there
the distance did not matter for her image
reached me unblurred by any atmosphere.

'Oh Lady, in whom my hope should ever soar
and who for my salvation suffered even
to set your feet upon Hell's broken floor,

'Through your power and your excellence alone
have I recognized the goodness and the grace
inherent in the things I have been showed'.

From Dante's *La Vita Nuova* II Commentary:

Nine times the heaven of the light had revolved in its own movement since my birth and had almost returned to the same point when the woman whom my mind beholds in glory first appeared before my eyes. She was called Beatrice by many who did not know what it meant to call her this. She had lived in this world for the length of time in which the heaven of the fixed stars had circled one twelfth of a degree towards the East. Thus, she had not long passed the beginning of her ninth year when she appeared to me and I was almost at the end of mine when I beheld her. She was dressed in a very noble color, a decorous and delicate crimson, tied with a girdle and trimmed in a manner suited to her tender age. The moment I saw her I say in all truth that the vital spirit, which dwells in the inmost depths of the heart, began to tremble so violently that I felt the vibration alarmingly in all my pulses, even the weakest of them. As it trembled, it uttered these words: *Ecce deus fortior me, qui veniens dominabitur mihi.* [Behold a god stronger than I, who coming shall rule over me.]

Sonnet XIV

Within my heart I sensed awaken
A loving spirit which slept
And from a distance Love then stepped
So happy, I felt almost mistaken.

He said, 'Think only of extending my fame.'
He laughed at each single word;
Then standing still by my side! my lord
Gazed back at the way whence he came.

I saw Giovanna and my lady Beatrice
Come up to where I was standing:
One wonder after another in show.
And as my memory repeats it like this,
Love told me: 'The first is called Spring;
The other's name is Love, she resembles me so.'

Canto XXXI

Beatrice has gone to Paradise on high
Among the angels in the realm of peace,
And you, ladies, she has left comfortless.
No quality of cold caused her to die,
Nor heat, as brings to others their release,
But only virtue and great gentleness.
For light, ascending from her lowliness,
So pierced the heavens with its radiance,
That God was moved to wonder at the same
And a sweet longing came
To summon to Him such benevolence;
And from on high He called her by her name,
Because our grievous life He saw to be
Unfit for such a noble thing as she.

Final paragraphs:

> A miraculous vision appeared to me, in which I beheld things which made me determine never to speak of that blessed lady until I could write worthily of her. To attain this end I study as hard as I can, as she knows in all truth. Therefore, if it pleases Him through whom all things live that my life may continue for a few years, I hope to write of her what has never been said of any woman.
>
> Then may it please God who is the Lord of Grace that my soul may rise to see the glory of its lady, who gazes in rapture on the face of Him "who is blessed throughout all ages".

The quotations from *La Vita Nuova* and Dante's *Paradiso* express clearly the nature of his love for Beatrice. His love was born in the earthly realm and gradually over the years, after her death, deepens until she becomes his guide in the spiritual world. From earthly love to sublime love is the path that Dante traversed in his journey. It is the story of his soul's initiation.

One question that might arise is why Beatrice, who apparently barely noticed Dante during her life, came so close to him after her death, as revealed in his visions. Are his visions merely the fancy of a poet's imagination? I propose not and suggest that instead we understand his visions as supersensible experiences. If we do, the veil can begin to fall from our eyes. We may understand his poetry as revealing profound spiritual experience. We may see that these two souls had a very strong karmic connection with one another. Such connections, developing over the course of time, are not necessarily lived out in full in each earthly existence. Instead, they may weave across the threshold between life in this world and in the supersensible world. Isn't it in fact remarkable that Beatrice means "the one who bestows blessing"? One might even wonder whether it would have been possible for Dante to compose one of the world's greatest poems without the inspiration of his beloved. By this inspiration, I mean not merely a rapturous swelling in the poet's breast but an actual working together of the two beings across the threshold of death. If one is willing to contemplate this possibility, one begins to discern the loftiness of the love about which we are speaking.

What does it mean when a human being is able to encompass the whole spectrum of *eros, philia,* and *agape* in one lifetime? Is it even possible? I think so. Just as the rose blossom gradually grows out of the manure and worm-infested soil, so love between man and woman can find a beginning in the carnal impulses of our instinctual natures and gradually rise through tenderness and affection to deep friendship and then on to reveal an eternal spiritual bond that survives after death.

3

Shakespeare and the Alchemy of Love

Of the world's most famous poets and playwrights, perhaps none penetrated so deeply into the mysteries of love as William Shakespeare. In his poems and plays he explored every aspect of the relationship between men and women, from the basest to the noblest.

Shakespeare was born on April 23, 1564, a day dedicated in the calendar of the saints to St. George, and died April 23, 1616. Legend tells us that St. George, guardian of England, saved a princess about to be sacrificed to a dragon that threatened the kingdom. St. George thus represents the savior of the human soul in peril. Shakespeare, too, could be seen as one thoroughly familiar with the soul life of humanity. We might call him an alchemist of the soul who through his works reveals a prodigious and warm-hearted understanding of every aspect of human nature and its transformation, how it responds under certain conditions, how it harmonizes with or repels others, and how through the course of time its development can be traced.

What is both strange and significant is that we know hardly anything of this great man's life, neither public nor private. It has been ascertained that at age eighteen he married Anne Hathaway who was eight years his senior, and that shortly after the wedding their first daughter Susanne was born. Three years later twins followed.

Though Shakespeare lived primarily in London from age twenty-three onward, he seems to have remained in close contact with his family in Stratford-upon-Avon. We also know that by the time he was thirty-three he was sufficiently well-off to buy a house, "New Place," in Stratford for Anne and his children.

Based in part on his sonnets, some critics propose that a "Dark Lady" existed in Shakespeare's life, though nothing is known about her with any certainty. What is clear is that William Shakespeare retired permanently to Stratford at the age of forty-nine to live the remaining three years of his life with his wife, and wrote his final testament on March 25, 1616, a few weeks before his death.

While it does not appear that Shakespeare led a tumultuous love-life, his one hundred and fifty sonnets, which represent some of the finest love poetry in the English language, explore many aspects of the relationship of men and women. Composed by him when he was between the ages of twenty-eight and thirty-five, the sonnets contain the full palette of love's many moods—rapture, betrayal, loss, sacrifice, fulfillment, despair, and suffering. In sonnet CXVI, the eternal quality of true love that lives beyond death is beautifully expressed:

> Let me not to the marriage of true minds
> Admit impediments. Love is not love
> Which alters when it alteration finds,
> Or bends with the remover to remove:
> O, no! it is an ever-fixed mark,
> That looks on tempests, and is never shaken;
> It is the star to every wandering bark,
> Whose worth's unknown, although his height be taken.
> Love's not Time's fool, though rosy lips and cheeks
> Within his bending sickle's compass come;
> Love alters not with his brief hours and weeks,
> But bears it out even to the edge of doom.
> If this be error, and upon me prov'd,
> I never writ, nor no man ever lov'd.

The sonnets alone constitute a remarkable alchemy of the loving soul in the immediate presence of the beloved. By the time we reach the seventeenth century in which Shakespeare lived, the Age of the Troubadours, when love was sung about in an idealized manner, was well past. Increasingly, from the Age of Elizabeth onward, love between men and women becomes personalized. Love awakens in an individual, intimate way in the hearts of the ones who fall in love, less and less determined by family and social standing, though it will still take some time before these bonds are fully loosened.

Shakespeare's early play, *Romeo and Juliet,* is a perfect example of two young people falling deeply in love, though their families are at enmity. The tragedy lies in the fact that the respective parents, the Montagues and Capulets, are still adhering to the blood line, unable to see that a new, personalized love bond has awakened in their children. The love of Romeo and Juliet, out of the fullness and purity of their hearts, leads them to the ultimate sacrifice of death, so that the feuds in Verona might cease and that peace and lasting reconciliation might ensue.

Very different is the mood in a later play composed when Shakespeare was forty-four years of age, Antony and Cleopatra. It is not only a powerful Roman historical drama but also the passionate love story of an aging, sensuous, and dissolute couple. Cleopatra, Queen of Egypt (who was actually Greek), was a woman of remarkable beauty:

> Age cannot wither her, nor custom stale
> Her infinite variety: other women cloy
> The appetites they feed: but she makes hungry
> Where most she satisfies . . .
>
> Act II, scene ii

She had many lovers, including Julius Caesar, who lived with her in Egypt and Rome before his assassination. Mark Antony in his sunset years, having led a dissolute life and fought many battles, is totally captivated by her allure. For a brief moment, he recognizes her true nature: "She is cunning past man's thought" (Act I, Scene ii). Yet, he is swept off his feet: "Eternity was in our lips and eyes"(Act I, Scene ii), and on her birthday he says, "Let's have one other gaudy night"(Act III, Scene ii). Because of his passion for her, Mark Antony throws his responsibilities as a general and Roman statesman to the four winds. When he is informed that Cleopatra has died, unaware that the news is false, he resolves to commit suicide by falling on his sword:

> Since Cleopatra died,
> I have liv'd in such dishonor, that the Gods
> Detest my baseness.
>
> Act IV, scene xiv

The fifth act of this poignant drama about a couple locked in a cloying, lascivious bond takes us through the death of Cleopatra, who, learning of Antony's suicide, puts an asp to her breast. They expire together. In this exotic play, Shakespeare portrays the workings of the basest passions in two characters who, had they fulfilled their true destinies, could have been models for the good of their people.

While his tragedies, comedies, and romances present love's many facets, from the darkest, lustful degradation, to the noblest light-filled sacrifice, Shakespeare never analyzes emotions with the scalpel of the psychologist. Shakespeare simply portrays the deeper recesses of the soul in the interaction of his characters. It would go beyond the framework of this presentation to consider some twenty plays in detail. Let it suffice to cite a few examples briefly so that the reader might examine these passages further.

Carnal degradation is powerfully portrayed in *Titus Andronicus*: a drama of rape, incest and betrayal. The same is found in *Cymbeline* in the character of the lascivious, uncouth Cloten whose love turned to lust. In *King Lear,* the evil daughters of the king, Goneril and Regan, conspire against their father, who is unable to perceive their dark intent; his paternal love is corrupted by greed. In *Othello,* Cassius cunningly weaves a web of fatal deception so that Othello, gnawed by an insatiable jealousy, is driven to murder his faithful wife Desdemona; love is driven by jealousy to murder.

On the light-filled side of the spectrum, we find some of the noblest characters, and especially a number of women come to mind. The self-sacrifice of King Lear's Cordelia, who truly loves her father; the nobility of Portia in *The Merchant of Venice;* and in *The Winter's Tale* the steadfast love of Hermione, who suffers the terrible public humiliations by her jealous husband, Leontes, and finally opens his eyes and redeems him.

Love at the three Greek levels is clearly exemplified in an early comedy with tragic overtones, *The Merchant of Venice.* The main plot revolves around Shylock, a money lender, and Antonio, a merchant unable to repay his debt to Shylock. The subplot beautifully woven into the fabric of the play culminates in three weddings at Belmont (*la belle montagne,* the beautiful mountain), overlooking the mercantile city of Venice. We have come to know Gratiano, a friend of Bassanio, the hero of the play, who tells us:

> Let me play the fool:
> With mirth and laughter let old wrinkles come,
> And let my liver rather heat with wine
> Than my heart cool with mortifying groans.
> Why should a man, whose blood is warm within,
> Sit like his grandsire cut in alabaster?
>
> Act I, scene i

He falls in love with Nerissa, the lady in waiting to Portia. Their warm, passionate union is at the level of the feeling-soul. Lorenzo, another friend of Bassanio, has become enamored with the beautiful Jessica, Shylock's daughter, who has eloped with him. When they arrive at Belmont, under a star-lit sky, to await the arrival of Portia, we hear one of the most beautiful love dialogues in Shakespeare. Their speeches are filled with allusions to famous lovers of the past, and when they turn to their own relationship, Lorenzo lifts Jessica's attention to the starry heavens. He is aware of the harmony of the spheres and their music:

> How sweet the moonlight sleeps upon this bank!
> Here will we sit, and let the sounds of music
> Creep in our ears; soft stillness and the night
> Become the touches of sweet harmony.
> Sit, Jessica. Look, how the floor of heaven
> Is thick inlaid with patines of bright gold:
> There's not the smallest orb which thou behold'st
> But in his motion like an angel sings,
> Still quiring to the young-eyed cherubins;

Such harmony is in immortal souls;
But whilst this muddy vesture of decay
Doth grossly close it in, we cannot hear it.
Act V, scene i

Theirs is a love not only sensual but lifted to a higher level of the soul, with feelings woven through with thoughts that illumine the relationship.

After many vicissitudes, Bassanio wins the hand of the steadfast Portia. Her father had decreed that the suitor who chose the right casket would win her. Instead of selecting the gold or silver one, Bassanio opens the lead casket, for he is prepared "to give and hazard all he has." There, he finds Portia's picture. Portia and Bassanio have recognized one another in their eternal essence, and their love is all the purer and nobler because of it. Their bond reaches the highest levels of soul where the loving will is woven into the thoughts and feelings they have for one another. This development has in it the making of an eternal bond that goes beyond death.

A final reflection in connection with Shakespeare—when Bassanio arrives in Belmont, to make his choice of a casket, music accompanies the ritual. It is significant that a song is heard which expresses in the form of a question the origin of love:

Tell me where is fancy bred,
Or in the heart or in the head?
How begot, how nourished?
Reply, reply.

It is engender'd in the eyes,
With gazing fed; and fancy dies
In the cradle where it lies.
Let us all ring fancy's knell:
I'll begin it.—Ding, dong, bell.
Ding , dong, bell.
Act III, scene ii

In modern English we would say, Where is the love born? Is love born in the heart or in the mind? In the feelings or in the thoughts? According to the words of the song it is engendered in the eyes and grows through gazing upon the beloved.

In the process of loving, heart, head, and eyes are all involved. In a later chapter we shall examine this further. Rudolf Steiner has pointed out that the lasting nature of love arises when thinking (ideas), feelings (heart), and willing (deeds) are in perfect harmony.

At about the same time that William Shakespeare was composing his last three plays, known as Romances, a profound esoteric work, *The Alchemical Wedding of Christian Rosenkreutz* (1604), appeared in Kassel, Germany. It narrates in seven days the initiation process of Christian Rosenkreutz. In its description of the fifth day of the initiation (a Wednesday, the day of the planet Mercury), the work includes a poem about love. In a series of six stanzas by means of question and answer the magic of love is described in a most sensitive, profound yet simple manner. The poem rises in stages from the love involved in procreation to the sublime love in spiritual union. It is here quoted in full.

Though written in the seventeenth century, it bears a reflection of our time and expresses valuable insights into the mystery of love.

Siren's Song

from Poem of the 5th day of
The Chemical Wedding of Christian Rosenkreutz

I

There's nothing better here below,
Than beauteous, noble Love,
Whereby we like to God do grow,
And none to grief do move.
Wherefore let's chant it to the King
That all the Sea thereof may ring.
We question; answer you.

II

What was it that at first us made?
　　'Twas Love.
And what hath Grace a fresh conveigh'd?
　　'Tis Love.
Whence was't (pray tell us) we were born?
　　Of Love
How came we then again forlorn?
　　Sans Love.

III

Who was it (say) that us conceived?
　　'Twas Love.
Who Suckled, Nursed, and Reliev'd?
　　'Twas Love.
What is it we to our Parents owe?
　　'Tis Love.
What do they us such kindness show?
　　Of Love.

IV

Who gets herein the Victory?
　　'Tis Love.
Can Love by search obtained be?
　　By Love.
How may a Man good works perform?
　　Through Love.
Who into one can two transform?
　　'Tis Love.

V

Then let our Song sound,
Till its Echo rebound.
To Loves honour and praise,
Which may ever increase
With our noble Princes, the King,
　　and the Queen,
The Soul is departed, their Body's within.

VI

And as long as we live,
God graciously give;
That as great Love and Amity,
They bear each other mightily;
So we likewise, by Love's own Flame,
May reconjoin them once again.

VII

Then this annoy
Into great Joy
(If many thousand younglings deign)
Shall change, and ever so remain.

It should be noted that Christian Rosenkreutz is regarded in mystery knowledge as one of the greatest initiates. The Alchemical Wedding describes in vivid imaginations one of the initiations of Christian Rosenkreutz during his long life in the fourteenth and fifteenth centuries (1378–1484). During this time, he worked essentially all over Europe and the Middle East, behind the scenes of external happenings.

4

Goethe—
The Search for the Eternal Feminine

> Love does not rule, does not dominate
> —it forms, it fashions and this is more.
>
> from *The Green Snake and the Beautiful Lily*

After sixty years of work on his monumental drama, *Faust,* Johann Wolfgang von Goethe (1749–1832) completed the masterpiece a few weeks before his death at the age of eighty-two. The last two lines of the Mystical Chorus that speaks at the end of the drama's second part express in a profound way Goethe's ideal conception of womanhood:

> The eternal feminine
> Draws us upwards.

Translated in various ways, including "draws us to perfection" and "lifts us into the heights," this line is radiant with meaning. It illuminates the ideal of love that Goethe upheld in his life. As his personal correspondence reveals, he continually strove toward a noble and sacred love, though rarely did he feel he attained it.

In Part I of *Faust* we find the following lines:

> Two souls, alas, are dwelling in my breast,
> And one is striving to forsake its brother.
> Unto the world in grossly living zest,
> With clinging tendrils, one adheres;
> The other rises forcibly in quest
> Of rarefied ancestral spheres.

Goethe felt deeply this two-foldness in himself and suffered from it throughout his life. While we know very little about Shakespeare the man, Goethe's life has been documented in practically every detail. We know what he did from day to day, due to his many letters, his journals, the descriptions he wrote of his journeys, particularly in Switzerland and Italy, and his many conversations with friends and secretaries. He embarked upon an autobiography, which covers the first twenty-six years of his life, when he was sixty. A remarkable document, it has been claimed by some critics to be the finest autobiography ever written. It bears the intriguing title, *Poetry and Truth*, which characterizes something of the inner nature of one of the greatest writers the world has ever known.

In spite of the many details we have regarding his everyday life, his relationships, and friendships, there is nevertheless in Goethe a certain reticence, a certain shyness, in spite of the fact that he is candid about the many connections that colored his long life, both with men and women. For instance, he tells us that at the age of fourteen, still a boy, he was deeply moved on meeting a young woman named Gretchen. It was his first conscious experience of womanhood and it moved him to the core, remaining with him as an ideal throughout his life. It is worthwhile to read of his experience in his own words:

> The form of that girl followed me from that moment on every path; it was the first durable impression which a female being had made upon me: and as I could find no pretext to see her at home, and would not seek one, I went to church for love of her, and had soon traced out where she sat. Thus, during the long Protestant service, I gazed my fill at her. When the congregation left the church, I did not venture to accost her, much less to accompany her, and was perfectly delighted if she seemed to have remarked me and to have returned my greeting with a nod. Yet I was not long denied the happiness of approaching her.

Later, he writes:

> The first propensities to love in an uncorrupted youth take altogether a spiritual direction. Nature seems to desire that one sex may by the senses perceive goodness and beauty in the other. And thus to me, by the sight of this girl—by my strong inclination for her—a new world of the beautiful and the excellent had arisen.
>
> *Poetry and Truth,* Part I, Book 5

This account is not of a youth's sexual awakening, but much more of an ideal, an almost religious element that he apprehended through this young girl a few years his senior. The relationship did not come to anything, but the experience marked him deeply, and we might imagine that it found its culmination in the last lines of the Mystical Chorus quoted above.

The young Goethe for a time belonged to the *Sturm und Drang* (Storm and stress) movement in German literature with a number of like-minded revolutionary friends. His was an intense inner struggle that, as with many youth, could erupt into his daily life. By the time he was twenty-six, his emotional turmoil had painfully affected three love affairs.

The first was with Frederica Brion, whom he loved deeply and who in turn was very attached to him. He must have proposed marriage, but at the last minute he withdrew, much to Frederica's chagrin. It broke her heart, and Goethe also suffered deeply from a separation that he felt was inevitable. This propensity to renounce marks a recurring trait of his character. He found it difficult to commit himself, in spite of the strength of his passion and feelings.

In the case of Charlotte Buff, the drama was even more profound. She was the bride of one of his friends. Goethe fell hopelessly in love with her, but in a situation that could have turned into a tragedy, he was wise enough to master his deep attachment, break from her, and once again renounce.

The drama of this relationship is reflected in his enormously popular novel, *The Sorrows of Young Werther,* written in the form of letters, at the end of which the hero commits suicide because of a desperate love triangle. This work made Goethe famous overnight, not only in German-speaking countries but in the whole of

Europe, for translations were made almost immediately after its publication. In fact, it caused a scandal by being seen as an influence upon numbers of young men to commit suicide after being rebuffed by the young women they were pursuing.

Next, Goethe fell in love with Lili Schonemann. She appears to have been a delightful young woman, attractive and vivacious. She captured his heart, and as the affair developed, they became engaged. However, once again before the marriage ceremony took place, Goethe withdrew. Lili had been prepared to follow him to America.

In the end destiny appeared in the form of an invitation Goethe received from the Grand Duke of Weimar, a small, prosperous, and cultured duchy in the heart of Germany. Goethe was twenty six. He had already achieved a reputation as an author and poet. In cultural circles he was well known.

On arriving in Weimar he met Charlotte von Stein, Lady in Waiting to the Duchess, seven years his senior, and married with seven children. She was a gracious, highly educated woman, with fascinating black eyes, although rather melancholic in temperament. She accepted the fact that her husband, who was in charge of the stables, was often away and that they did not share the same interests. At thirty-three, she could not envisage that the future held anything new for her.

Everything for her changed radically upon Goethe's arrival, however. He was handsome and artistic. He had a wonderful way with women and men alike. From the first moment they met, Goethe and Charlotte fell deeply in love with one another. We recall an earlier mention in this book of a poem that Goethe wrote on the evening of their first meeting when he wondered whether in a previous life she had not been his sister, or whether they had been man and wife.

This profound experience of meeting someone known in a previous life resonated deeply in both souls. They felt that they were destined for one another. Over time, the relationship developed into what one might call a loving friendship that lasted, with ups and downs, for some sixteen years. Accessible today is the voluminous correspondence between them. Goethe wrote no less than one thousand seven hundred letters to Charlotte, in addition to many poems dedicated to her. She is present, as well, behind characters of uprightness and true love in several of his plays. We do not have any of Charlotte's letters to Goethe, but we can surmise how deep their relationship became over the years.

In spite of her own strong feelings and his passionate advances, Charlotte always kept the relationship within bounds, although they saw one another nearly every day for a meal or conversations in the garden. There is no reason to believe that the intimacy became physical. She was his muse, his friend, the loved one whom he had always known, and who was to become also his mentor. She helped refine his manners to meet court standards and his speech, which still carried a Frankfurt accent.

Although the Weimar court initially disapproved of the relationship, the friendship was eventually accepted socially. As a result, Goethe and Charlotte often attended the various musical and theatrical entertainments together. We should remember that Weimar at that time received royalty as well as famous composers, writers, and poets, and that in nearby Jena was one of the most famous universities in Europe. Goethe was on friendly terms with Charlotte von Stein's husband. As well, he became a mentor to Charlotte's oldest son, who came to live with him and became his traveling companion.

Although his relationship with Charlotte was flourishing, when Goethe was thirty-eight he determined to explore Italy on his own and slipped away from Weimar surreptitiously. One day in September he set forth under the assumed name of Phillip Mueller in a large coach that contained a bed and a desk, together with his coachman. He did not inform his friends, and even Charlotte had no idea where he had gone. Weeks passed before she received a sign of life from him.

Goethe felt reborn in Italy. The sunny Mediterranean lifestyle with all of its fascinations developed him as an independent man and artist. He considered becoming a painter, even after the many poems and plays he had written, for he was gifted in that art also.

In Rome he found an expatriate colony of Germans whose company he enjoyed. He lived among the painters and delighted in meeting Italians for he spoke the language fluently. And he fell passionately in love with a young Roman woman of great beauty. They became lovers. His life in Italy included a deep, erotic experience reflected in poems titled "Roman Elegies," which he composed after his nearly two-year stay. Though never crude, they portray the uninhibited and tender relationship with his Roman mistress.

When Goethe returned to Weimar, to the somber north and the narrow confines of the court, he was a changed man. It took his friends quite a time to adjust. Charlotte was cool toward him, perhaps surmising what had occurred in Rome.

To make matters even more acute for his friends all around, shortly after his return a new woman entered his life. A buxom country girl, Christiane Vulpius came to visit the prestigious privy councilor and cabinet minister—for these were Goethe's official positions—to seek his help in granting a favor for her brother. They were attracted to one another, he the famous, highly educated writer, poet, and statesman and she, a simple, almost illiterate girl from the country. Within a very short time she became his mistress and they began living together.

We can imagine that their relationship shocked the community, not necessarily because Goethe had a mistress but particularly because she was a simple country girl, utterly unacceptable in court circles. She proved to be a loving companion, looking after Goethe with love and affection, and they had five children together, of which only one survived. It was after sixteen years, when Christiane literally saved Goethe's life during the Napoleonic wars, that they decided to marry. Their teenage son was present at the ceremony. Little by little Christiane was accepted. She had a kindly, affectionate nature that won the hearts of many.

We can hardly imagine a greater contrast between the two women who influenced Goethe's life so profoundly: Charlotte von Stein, sophisticated, highly educated, speaking several languages, and Christiane, a country girl with practically no education, warm hearted with a cheerful disposition. Christiane had little inkling of the extent of her husband's genius, that he was considered by some to be on a par with Homer, Dante, and Shakespeare. She was unable to take any serious interest in his writings, whereas Charlotte had been the first to hear, read, and comment on whatever Goethe composed.

In his life in Weimar after Italy, Goethe and Charlotte met from time to time, but their relationship was strained and formal. In old age they appeared to reconcile and discover some embers that had remained of their former intensity, though the tone in their letters never went beyond his "Dear Friend" and her "Dear Privy Councilor." Charlotte died before Goethe in her eighties.

In his great drama, *Faust*, Goethe explores the power of love. He tackles the theme of man's forming a partnership with the dark powers. Dr. Faustus is a university professor in his fifties who has studied every discipline, including philosophy, medicine, and theology, and yet feels that he knows nothing of the deeper forces that move the world. In his longing to experience the secret force of the universe, he makes a pact with Mephistopheles. The devil offers him the opportunity to become thirty years younger and enjoy all of the sensual pleasures in which he had never indulged. Alcohol proves to be no temptation for Dr. Faustus, but when he is led to the witches' kitchen and given a drug, he becomes an easy prey to the forces of evil. Shown in a vision the image of Helen of Troy, the most beautiful woman of antiquity, he immediately wishes to possess her. Mephistopheles assures him that with this potion in his belly, he will see Helen in every woman.

As Faust steps into the street, still reeling from the powerful draft that he has just drunk, he sees the young, innocent, lovely Gretchen, and wishes at all cost to possess her. His lust has been awakened, and the consequences are disastrous. The drama describes how he seduces the young Gretchen. In the process he becomes guilty of her mother's death. Then, he kills Gretchen's brother. She drowns her child, in prison loses her mind, and is executed for the murder of her baby.

In the midst of this tragedy, Goethe shows a gradual transformation in Faust from raw, sexual lust to a budding love for Gretchen. It is brought about by Gretchen's love for him. For while Mephistopheles does everything he can to prevent anything good from arising in their relationship, Gretchen loves Faust in spite of the way he treats her and the devastation he wreaks in her life. This love grows spiritually to the extent that after her death, Gretchen saves Faust from the grasp of Mephistopheles.

After these dramatic events, Faust still has many years to live and tragic ordeals to face. We find him at the end of Part II, one hundred years old, blind, and accompanied by Worry. As he dies, entering spiritual worlds, Gretchen approaches from the heavens and through her sacrificial, loving intercession, she redeems his guilt laden soul. It is at this point that we find the words, "The eternal feminine draws us upwards."

We can trace a golden thread through everything Goethe did in his life. It is the depiction of the metamorphosis of love through the levels of *eros, philia,* and *agape*. This transformation requires renunciation and sacrifice. The mature Goethe expressed it with great simplicity in a poem from the collection of *West-East, Divan*:

> Dying and becoming.
> If you do not have this,
> You are but a somber guest
> On the darkling earth.

Goethe struggled all of his life to transform the old so that it might be born anew at a higher level. He was confident that human beings, if they but strove and learned to discipline their inner forces, were capable of realizing the finest ideal of humanity.

> Let man and woman be noble,
> Helpful and good!
> For that alone
> Distinguishes him
> From all beings
> That we know.

Goethe was a profound Christian soul, although clearly his was not a traditional Christian path. He was no churchgoer, though he immersed himself again and again in the Bible, both the Old and New Testaments. He was, rather, engaged in exploring the great themes of evil, death, and love. What he found was that love has redemptive power. His was a remarkable, independent journey through life that engaged with the deepest Christ-Mystery.

5

Novalis
Finding the Beloved beyond Death

Our theme of love is reflected in an especially brilliant facet by Friederich von Hardenberg, called Novalis (May 2, 1772–March 25, 1801) the great German poet and an architect of German Romanticism. One of eleven children, he was sickly and suffered from serious illnesses as a child, which he appears to have overcome at puberty. He emerged as a remarkably gifted young man, studying law at the University of Jena in Germany and history under Friedrich von Schiller (1759–1805), the renowned playwright and poet who was a close friend of Goethe. Novalis so admired Schiller that friends said he defended Schiller against all detractors "with the fiery zeal of an Elijah."

In 1793 when he was twenty-one, Novalis met Friedrich Schlegel (1772–1829), who remained one of his closest friends for the rest of his life. Schlegel, the philosopher, critic, and writer who provided the Romantic movement with a strong psychological basis, encouraged Novalis in his writing. After study at the universities of Leipzig and Wittenberg, at twenty-two Novalis passed his bar exam and graduated with an additional degree as an actuary.

It was then that destiny met him in the beautiful Sophie von Kuehn, a delightful girl of twelve with whom he fell deeply in love. Immediately, she became the joy of his life, the inspiration for his work. Although theirs was an idyllic and chaste relationship, the difference in their ages made it highly unusual. They eventually became engaged in secret, but within two years Sophie died at the age of fifteen in 1797. Her passing shocked the twenty-five-year-old Novalis to the core. One day when in utter despair, Novalis visited Sophie's grave, and, as he writes of it, he experienced a profound, inner transformation akin to an initiation in worlds beyond the grave. Sophie came to him in all of her spiritual splendor. For the remainder of his brief life, his creative, poetic powers were quickened under her inspiration as he explored the mysteries of the night, which we may understand as the mysteries of death. He came to see that a relationship with one who has died can be developed each night during sleep and brought to consciousness during the day. He explored his experiences in this realm in his famous *Hymns to the Night* (1800). He went on to write poetry that continues to rank among the finest in the German language, including *The Spiritual Songs* (1802). His prose work, *Christendom or Europe* (1826), is still printed in German anthologies. Also notable is his novel, *Henry von Ofterdingen* (1802), which tells the story of a legendary minnesinger whose wanderings in search of a "blue flower" became a prominent symbol in the German Romantic movement.

As his inner life deepened, in his daily life Novalis pursued studies in a mining academy, studying under a prominent geologist, Abraham Gottlob Werner, who became a friend. He eventually secured a position in a salt works. He met Goethe on two occasions, visiting him in Weimar, though it appears that no close relationship developed between them. In fact, Goethe did not take to the young Romantic movement, and equally Novalis seems to have taken little interest in Goethe's strivings. Goethe did once meet the youthful Sophie von Kuehn and remarked on her angelic disposition.

Novalis eventually developed a loving relationship with Julie von Charpentier. He met often with the Romantic poets living around Jena, one of the key cities in which the movement flourished.

Novalis' most compelling written work for many readers is the three volumes of *Fragments,* a collection of his inspired thoughts on almost every subject under the sun: mathematics, physics, medicine, geology, philosophy, psychology, philology and art, states and human patterns, cosmology, religion, insights into human affairs, and the future of the universe. These thoughts were meant to serve as notes for a tremendous enterprise he had conceived: a universal encyclopedia.

Novalis aspired to what he called in *Fragments* "magical idealism," a phrase he coined during the last years of his life. What he meant exactly by it is difficult to describe. He called it a new faculty of perception or thinking that could transform the commonplace into the lofty. It is a faculty born out of the heart and intimately connected with love. In fact, in one of the passages in *Fragments* we read, "Love is the basis for the possibility of magic. Love works in a magical way." This magic could transform the world and lift it to a new stage of perfection.

All of his projects and plans were left uncompleted when, at age twenty-nine, Novalis died of tuberculosis. The morning of his death, he had taken breakfast, requested some books, and asked his brother Carl to play the piano. He passed away peacefully as the sun reached its zenith. A close friend, Ludwig Tieck, a fellow poet, wrote later that Novalis looked like John the Evangelist "with his light brown locks and the fiery, shining eyes, with his wise, almost transparent forehead and his slender form."

We may now turn to his words themselves to create the mood of his explorations. From *Fragments* we read:

> The world must be romanticized. In this way one rediscovers its original meaning. Romanticizing is nothing but a qualitative raising to a higher power. In this operation the lower self becomes identified with a higher self. Just as we ourselves are such a qualitative, exponential series. This operation is still wholly unknown.

On birth and death:

> Whoever does not reach perfection here perhaps will reach it over there or else will have to begin an earthly career over again. Could there be a death over there, the result of which would be birth on earth?...Do not I myself choose all my destinies from eternity?

A telling passage from *Henry von Ofterdingen*:

> The earth lay before him like a dear old home that after a long absence he found again. Thousands of memories awoke in him...

—Since I left the grave
—Did you die once before?
—How else could I live?
—How does it happen that you know me?
—Oh, from olden times.

Of all his poetic works, *Hymns to the Night* may be the most profound. It is a poem in free verse, combined with prose passages, that falls into six unequal sections. Several aspects of it are close to our theme. The first hymn begins with a song in praise of light. It is only if one penetrates to night, which is the mother of all things, the herald of sacred worlds, that one can begin to fathom the mysteries of the world. Light is the creator of all things, and night is maternal wisdom, whose daughter is love.

The second hymn sings the praises of sleep. The unawakened one knows sleep as but a shadow, yet to those who have uncovered the sacred quality of sleep, it holds the key to life itself. Novalis alludes here to something not easy to grasp. Love has stages, degrees. Ultimately, one is related to the other as spirit to spirit, a connection that can be found fully beyond the threshold, that is, in the world of sleep, or in the realm of death.

The third hymn is a deeply personal one. It portrays Novalis' despair at the loss of Sophie and the day he came to her grave when the boundaries of birth and death were torn asunder. The self is reborn, and in an inward vision, the speaker of the hymn tells of grasping the hands of his beloved. This night experience is more than a dream, for now he is able to join his beloved. He writes:

> Once, when I poured out bitter tears, when, dissolved in pain, scattered, and I was standing alone at the barren mound that hid the figure of my life in its narrow, dark space—alone, as no one could be more alone, driven by unspeakable anxiety—strengthless, with just one thought left of need. As I looked around for help, could not move forward and not backward, and hung onto the fleeting, extinguished life with infinite craving, then came from blue distances—for the heights of my old blessedness,

> a twilight shiver—and with one stroke my birth's bond ripped—Light's chains. There the earthly splendor fled and my sadness with it—misery flowed into a new, unplumbed world—You, Night-inspiration, heaven's sleep, came over me—the region lifted gently up; over the region my released and newborn spirit floated. The hill became a cloud of dust—through the cloud I saw the transfigured features of my beloved. In her eyes rested the forever—I took her hands, and my tears were a glittering and unrippable bond. Years by the thousands flew off to the distance, like storms. In her embrace I wept overjoyed tears at the new life.—It was the first and the only dream—and only since then I've felt an unchangeable, eternal faith in the heaven of Night and its Light, the beloved.

Clearly, we have here a profound and personal initiation experience, which through the inner death and despair of the poet leads to new life, to resurrection. The love that he has always felt for Sophie is now quickened all the more. Sophie guides his seeking soul across the threshold to a meeting with the Christ Being. This meeting is expressed in a most wonderful way in the subsequent segments of this remarkable poem. The fourth hymn opens, "Now I know when the final morning will be—when the light no longer frightens away the night and love—when sleeping will be forever just one unspendable dream." A little later in the same hymn, Novalis speaks of love being the "daughter of the night."

To find another art form as deep and sensitive in its evocation of such a mood, one would have to look at the paintings of Raphael. The Renaissance painter above all other subjects depicted Mary and the Child with a beauty and profundity that remains through the ages. Yet, this Mary represents the Sophia, as well—the "eternal feminine," as Goethe called her at the end of his *Faust*.

Finally, most directly, a number of the fragments in Novalis's work are entitled, "Sophie, or On Woman." Let me quote a few of them to add color to our picture.

The heart is the key to the world and to life. One lives in this helpless condition in order to love and to meet other obligations. Through incompleteness one becomes susceptible to other influences, and to assimilate those strange influences is the aim. In sickness only should and can others help us. So Christ is from this point of view, certainly, the key to the world.

Love is the design of universal history—the Amen of the universe.

There is only one temple in the world, and that is the human body. Nothing is holier than this high Form. One touches heaven when one touches a human body.

Woman is the symbol of good and beauty; man is the symbol of truth and right.

Rightly can many a woman say that she "sinks" into the arms of her lover. Wealth to those who into their lover's arms "rise."

From *Pollen* and *Fragments*
translated by Arthur Versluis

Novalis's initiation experience at the grave of his beloved deeply influenced everything he wrote during the remaining four years of his life. From across the threshold she was constantly present, and he felt her sacred inspiration. While the totality of his works is a mere four volumes—he was by no means prolific—everything he wrote is like a polished jewel.

In fact, Novalis's work has the quality of a seed. Although he died two hundred years ago, his impulse remains substantially enigmatic, hardly understood. That is because it is an impulse for the future. He points to the necessity for an inwardness of soul, for inner transformation, without which we shall be unable to grow close to Christ and to one another.

For Novalis, love is lifted from the earthly into the *agape* of an indestructible, eternal union with a beloved even beyond the threshold of death.

6

Vladimir Soloviev in Search of the Holy Sophia

Vladimir Soloviev's father was one of Russia's most influential professors of history, who had a marked western outlook. He seemed to be a typical scholar, absorbed in books, and aloof. The boy respected him but apparently there was little affection between the two.

His mother, from southern Russia, was an emotional, warm-hearted, somewhat shy and self-effacing person, highly imaginative and endowed with a delightful sense of humor. She loved poetry and displayed the typical, mystical tendencies of Eastern Europe.

In Vladimir Soloviev (1853–1900) both his father's and mother's tendencies can clearly be traced. He was a scholar, a profound mystic, a philosopher, a poet, a critic, and an enthusiast. He was popular, though lonely, and lived in society among professors, princes, ladies in waiting, students, nihilists, Jesuits, bishops, beggars, and coachmen. Everyone, without exception, including children and animals, sensed the enormous, radiant power of this extraordinary individuality. With no family beyond his parents, he lived with friends or in hotel rooms during the whole of his life.

Soloviev was a most handsome man, and once seen he was never forgotten. He was gifted with words and charmed all with whom he engaged in conversation. To women whom he loved most deeply, Soloviev wrote wonderful poetry, clearly expressing in his verses his perception of their higher selves. Yet, the women in his life never returned his love and seemed to have found him difficult to get on with.

Two powerful experiences coincided in the boy's early life. When he was nine years old, on Ascension Day, during the orthodox service in the chapel of Moscow University, he experienced the spiritual being of the Sophia, the Mother of the Universe, the Soul of the World. He wrote about his experience in a poem, "Flowers from the Meadow of Paradise in Her Hand." It was also at this time that seeing a young girl of his own age, he fell deeply in love in a childlike way reminiscent of Dante when he saw Beatrice for the first time. He carried these experiences deeply in his soul for the rest of his life.

As a boy, Soloviev was devout, yet he turned to atheism when he reached puberty. He lost his faith, burned his icons, and felt more closely connected to his father's views. At fifteen, a brilliant student, he studied mathematics and physics at Moscow University, in addition to philosophy and history. Darwinism became his new religion.

By the time he turned nineteen, however, he reconverted to Christianity and developed an interest in the writings of the Church fathers: St. Augustine, Jacob Boehme, and Paracelsus. After graduating at twenty, he enrolled at the Theological Academy where he mastered the entire range of western philosophy and the teachings of the Eastern Church fathers.

At the age of twenty-two, Soloviev received a scholarship to study at the British Museum in London. It is interesting to note that Karl Marx frequented the museum's reading room at this time. It was in that room that a second, life-changing experience of the Sophia was granted Soloviev. In that experience, he understood her to convey that she would reveal herself fully to him in Egypt at the foot of the pyramids. With one immediate, direct intent, he unhesitatingly responded to her call and left London, heading straight for the Egyptian desert. There, this tall, thin man in his dark, formal outfit paced the desert sands until, as had been promised, Sophia appeared to him for a third time.

Not only did he experience these profound spiritual events, eventually he shared them with the world, composing a long poem later in his life, when he was forty-five, titled "Three Encounters." This poem belongs to one of the most moving, visionary experiences ever captured in words. Interestingly, Soloviev intersperses its profound passages with humorous touches, quite intentionally to protect its subject from the mocking intellect.

The following extracts might convey something of the profound, spiritual experiences that informed Soloviev's striving during the last twenty-four years of his life and that culminated in the short story of the Anti-Christ.

Extracts from "Three Encounters"

Moscow—London—Egypt
Thrice you revealed yourself to sight of man,
Not in Shadowy imaginings of the mind;
In prophetic joy, in help, in grace vouchsafed,
To my soul's call your image came in answer.

—

The first time,—how long ago it was!
Thirty-six years have passed away since as a child
I felt the first burning darts of sudden love,
All confused and baffled by darkening clouds.

—

So ran my thoughts, when in the Service
On Ascension Day my soul was stirred with anger;
"All Earthly cares. . . to lay aside. . . in peace serene."

—

Enwoven with gold-blue, in streaming light,
Bearing still a flower from far-distant lands
Beckoning to me, you stand with radiant smile,
And then, as silently, you vanish from my sight.

After his childhood experience at the age of nine, we now turn to his stay in London.

It was not Paris, gay center of the world,
Nor dreamy Spain, nor glamorous Far Eastern lands,
The British Museum was my long journey's goal,
Nor indeed were my dreams and hopes deceived.

—

Most of the time I was alone in the great Library,
And, believe it or not, but God is my witness:
Mysterious powers led me to choose for reading
Everything possible concerning Her.

—

Once in days of Autumn I said to her, O Flower divine,
I feel your presence here! But why
Have you not appeared to me since childhood?

Hardly had I thought these words
When suddenly all was filled with golden azure,
And you were there in heavenly radiance;
There I saw your face, your face alone!

—

I said to her, you once let me see your face,
But your noble image I yet long to see;
The gift you granted to a child,
To a grown-up man you'll surely not refuse!

Within me now I heard the message: "Be in Egypt!"
To France then, and to Southern countries lies my road;
My feelings struggled not at all with reason,
And reason—like one dumb—said not a word.

—

Having arrived in Egypt, he paced up and down in front of the pyramids in the noonday heat, still dressed in the formal attire of a British gentleman, clothes specially purchased in England: a formal frock coat, silk top hat, and an umbrella. He had spent all his money and lived on credit. He was convinced that the Sophia would reveal herself to him. Bedouins mistook him for a devil, and after a frightening episode finally released him. And here follows his experience of the Sophia:

O radiant Countenance, you have not deceived me!
Your fullest glory I beheld amid the desert waste;

Ever will your heavenly roses bloom within me
Where'er my stream of life may flow. -
It lingered but a moment, then the vision faded,
The sun rose glorious upon the eastern sky;
The silent desert spread around me; my soul was
praying
To the blessed sound of chiming bells within.

—

My spirit wakens now, and here around me,
Arises once again the azure mist, as long ago,
While the sea of earthly life, conquered by your
beauty,
In silence has receded, far away.

There can be no doubt that Soloviev was graced by a profound experience of the Holy Sophia. She imparted her *agape* love to him, quickening and inspiring the rest of his life. While materialism gained ground in the world about him, he moved in the direction of the spiritual with all the greater ardor and consciousness.

What was the message imparted to him by the Sophia? To answer, we must follow the golden thread of his destiny from then onward.After his return to Moscow he was appointed to a leading position as university lecturer. In 1881 Czar Alexander II, known as the liberator, who was very much loved and admired, was murdered, to the great dismay of the Russian people. The culprit was found and Alexander III gave orders for his execution. Soloviev attempted to intervene. He wrote a letter to the Czar and begged him to spare the man's life. He wrote against capital punishment, saying that it was both unChristian and inhumane. The Czar responded publicly by saying that the man who requested leniency must have been out of his mind. As a result Soloviev was removed from his position at the university.

From then on, Soloviev became increasingly misunderstood. He began to work actively at what he called the unification of Christendom. He traveled to Paris, Vienna, and Croatia speaking with prelates and bishops and ministers of various faiths, awakening them to the importance of Christ's message of love, union and compassion. Yet, adversarial vicious powers came against him. He was accused of being Roman Catholic when he longed only for Rome to open its heart both to Protestantism and to the Orthodox Russian Church. Although disappointed that these religious leaders did not understand the true meaning of his appeals to them, Soloviev never lost his kindliness. One who did understand him was Fyodor Dostoyevski, the novelist, who was an intimate friend, and whom he deeply loved.

Soloviev found companionship in other ways, as well. From his earliest years, particularly in his poetry, he spoke of the relationship he had established with the dead. In fact, apparently he regularly conversed with those who had passed over the threshold.

His final work, "Conversations About War and Christianity," culminates in the short, visionary story about the coming of the Antichrist. A character, Mr. Z, finds a document and reads it to an assembled group. The document opens with remarkable prophecies about events in the twentieth century, which had hardly been anticipated in Soloviev's time. Among other things, the document declares that there will be a decisive struggle with the Muslim world, that Palestine (Israel) will become an autonomous nation, that there will be wars and conflicts encompassing the whole world including Asia and the United States, that the French will be driven from Tonkin and Siam, the English from Burma and the whole of India. It also foresees that in Europe in the twenty-first century a union would arise of more or less democratic states, which would be known as the United States of Europe.

The narrative continues, telling about a man of extraordinary talent, a great thinker, writer and social reformer who at the age of thirty-three would become a type of messiah. He believed in the good, but beneath all his good thoughts was prepared only to serve himself. A demon had entered into him and he said of himself: "Christ came before me: I appeared next, but that which appears later in time is in reality first. I shall come last at the end of history, exactly because I am the absolute and final savior. The first Christ is my forerunner. His mission was to prepare and make ready for my appearance."

This emperor-superman gradually becomes ruler of the world after various conflicts end, bringing his peace. At first the Antichrist is acclaimed as a great savior. However, gradually the leaders of the three Christian denominations—the Venerable John, head of the Russian Orthodox Church, Pope Peter II, head of the Roman Catholic Church, and Doctor Ernst Pauli, head of the Protestant congregation—and a small gathering of followers of the three see through the machinations of the Antichrist who operates with a magician from the East at his side.

When the Antichrist is unmasked, he brings down thunder and lightening from the heavens, killing both the Venerable John and Pope Peter. Doctor Pauli arranges for the two men to be carried from Jerusalem to the desert, where they are brought back to life. Dr. Pauli joins hands with the Venerable John and Pope Peter and the union of the three churches is thereby sealed. This represents the ideal for which Soloviev always strove.

The Antichrist is defeated, and all behold a wonder in heaven, a woman clothed in the sun, standing on a crescent moon with a crown of twelve stars upon her head. It is with this healing vision of the Sophia that the narrative abruptly ends. We hear that some pages appear to be missing, and it is on this note that this remarkable prophecy relating to the twenty-first century comes to a conclusion.

The appearance of the Sophia represents a culmination of Soloviev's profound conviction that the peace of the world is found in the Eternal Feminine. That this work was written a few months before his death in 1900 is of special significance. We recall that Rudolf Steiner spoke of the year 1899 as marking the end of Kali Yuga, a dark age that had lasted for 5,000 years, roughly since the building of the pyramids in Egypt. From 1900 onward, humanity is living in a Light Age in which gradually the light of the spirit will increasingly emerge in the consciousness of human beings everywhere. Soloviev's final work presages not only the advent of the Antichrist but also the healing intercession of a new Christ revelation and its radiant manifestation in the blessed presence of Mary Sophia.

One other work of Soloviev's must be mentioned. When he was forty, he wrote a small book entitled, *The Meaning of Love,* which surprisingly enough throws quite a different light on what we have discussed so far. One might have thought that his view on love would be mainly of a mystical, ideal nature. This book reveals quite the opposite. Soloviev attributes considerable importance to the sexual aspect of love, while being clear that sex is only one facet. Toward the end of this work he mentions the Symposium by Plato, who discerned the difference between Aphrodite Urania, the heavenly or spiritual Venus, and Aphrodite Pandemos, the earthly or human Venus. The ideal for Soloviev was embodied in the union of the two, in which the heavenly, eternal feminine would be made manifest in the reality of womanhood on earth.

In conclusion, the following quotation from *The Meaning of Love* throws further light on our topic:

> The meaning and worth of love as a feeling is that it really forces us, with all our being, to acknowledge for another the same absolute significance which, because of the power of egoism, we are conscious of only in our own selves. Love is important, not only as one of our feelings but as the transfer of all our interest in life from ourselves to another, as the shifting of the very center of our lives.

Note: I wish to express special indebtedness to Paul Allen for his book, *Vladimir Soloviev, Russian Mystic* (Steinerbooks), Eugenia Gouvitch for *Vladimir Soloviev, The Man and the Prophet* (Rudolf Steiner Press), and Peter Waage for *Der Unsichtbare Kontinent* (Verlag Freies Geistesleben-Stuttgart).

7

A Contemporary View

Having considered a few historical and literary examples of how love between man and woman has developed over the ages since Plato, we noticed that the great mystery of human attraction is many-layered and complex. We might agree that no emotion, no sentiment in human relations can create so much happiness, so much joy, and so much contentment as love. On the other hand, a relationship lacking the harmony and compatibility that love can bring causes the greatest pain, the greatest suffering, and the greatest desolation. Moreover, as we have seen in ancient Greece, love expresses itself in different realms of experience. There is *eros*, which is mainly associated with physical or sexual love; *philia*, which is related to friendship in both souls; and *agape*, which may be considered as the highest, most sublime form of love, that of a human being toward the Godhead, for example.

Let us now consider this ladder of love in contemporary life. If we focus our discussion on the relationships between a man and a woman, we then must ask if the very nature of a human being brings light to these levels of love. What is the nature of the human being? The answer to that could be a book in itself. Human nature as characterized by Rudolf Steiner (1861–1925)—a scientist, seer, educator and artist, who also devoted many years to medical research—has proved especially helpful to my research into this area.

Already early in the twentieth century, in 1904, Rudolf Steiner wrote the book, *Theosophy*, (which, incidentally, has nothing to do with the Theosophical Society). The title's meaning comes from the Greek words *theos* and *sophia*, which translate as "wisdom of the Gods." Yet, to fully comprehend this meaning, one must also understand that the wisdom of the Gods is none other than the wisdom of man.

In this basic book, Steiner characterizes the human as a being of body, soul, and spirit. Carefully viewed, the body consists of both matter and life. This interpenetrating body of life forces Steiner often referred to as the etheric body. The spirit of the human being, he writes, is the I AM, which comes from the great, eternal I AM. It is unique in each individual. The soul of the human being is that which acts as a mediator between the eternal and the transient. The soul expresses itself through three soul forces: thinking, feeling, and willing. It is influenced from birth to death by the transient bodily nature and always by the eternal I AM that dwells in our spiritual nature.

This recognition of the threefold human being is one of the most important contributions that Steiner has made to an understanding of our destiny on earth and our life after death. Reaching even further, it throws light on our prenatal condition before we actually incarnated in a body of flesh. For the sake of simplicity, we might say that in the birth of a child two streams are interwoven in a most complex manner. On the one hand, the child is influenced by his heredity and surroundings; on the other hand, by the stream of his spiritual nature, which goes back to his prenatal life in the spiritual world and previous embodiments on earth. It is especially this awareness of reincarnation and, with it, of karma that enables us to lift the veil on the true nature of love.

In Theosophy, Rudolf Steiner writes that although the human being is one entity, we can nevertheless discern nine parts that constitute this oneness. Number one is the physical body; number two, the etheric body or body of formative life forces. A third is called the astral body. It contains all our wishes, passions and aspirations. It is, one could say, a soul body that expresses through the three soul forces. The sentient soul, our fourth member, is the soul primarily expressing itself through our feeling life. The fifth member is called the intellectual or mind soul, which expresses itself through our reasoning powers that also contain an aspect of our feelings. The third soul force and sixth member is the consciousness soul, which observes objectively and, still in the process of being developed, consciously experiences the spiritual. Next unfold three higher forces of soul and spirit, which are present in most of us only in potential. The first of these higher soul forces, or the seventh member of the human being, is called spirit self or Manas, which arises as the astral body of desires is purified. The eighth member and second of the higher soul forces is called life spirit or Buddhi. It arises from the transformation of the etheric body. Finally, the ninth member and third higher soul force is called spirit man or Atman. It eventually emerges as the transformed physical body.

9. Atman or Spirit Man 8. Buddhi or Life Spirit 7. Manas or Spirit Self	Spirit
6. Consciousness Soul 5. Intellectual or Mind Soul 4. Sentient Soul	Soul
3. Astral Body 2. Etheric or Life Body 1. Physical Body	Body

In the nine-fold characterization of the human being, the I AM is active through the soul forces. The human being can also be characterized in a seven-fold manner in which the I AM dwells in the center.

7. Atman or Spirit Man
6. Buddhi or Life Spirit
5. Manas or Spirit Self
4. I AM
3. Astral Body
2. Etheric or Life Body
1. Physical Body

It should be understood that the bodies or sheaths above the physical body are all of a supersensible nature, yet reflect their influences within the physical, for example, in the way we behave, through our temperament, or the character we display.

The emergence of the three higher stages depends on our inner development. Rudolf Steiner indicated in his book *How to Know Higher Worlds* (1904) how these higher capacities of the soul could be developed through the work of the I AM on our lower sheaths. For instance, the purification of our astral body into spirit self would result in a person having direct insight into the world of revelations and the birth of a higher self. When in time the etheric body is transformed, the power of healing would be born. When in the distant future the human being transforms his physical body, the capacity of spirit man will arise, which would express itself in the highest form of sacrifice, namely, that a person lays down his life for another. Until now, only Christ Jesus himself has attained this level when out of infinite love for humanity He completely sacrificed Himself.

These considerations can help us understand reincarnation and karma. The following is only a brief resume of what Steiner described in his book *Theosophy* (1902) in a chapter on the topic, where the reader will find an encompassing discussion.

For our purpose it is sufficient to say that every incarnating soul brings with it a prenatal life and also the results of previous incarnations. The process of incarnation is a very complex one. The human I AM, together with the workings of the Hierarchies, gathers an astral body and an etheric body. The physical body is provided by the parents.

The baby gradually unfolds into childhood, youth, adolescence, maturity, middle age, and old age. If we learn to observe the biographical stages of each individual, we notice that gradually his or her karma, that is, destiny and relationships with other human beings, unfolds in joy or sorrow, in health or illness, in good fortune or bad luck. After death, a complex process severs us from our bodily constitution. We view our etheric body, which contains all our memories like an expanding panorama, for about three days. At that point, our astral body begins to detach itself. We then enter a purification period (called *kama loca* in Sanskrit) where we experience our life in reverse, from the moment of death to the moment of birth, in such a way that we experience the impact of our actions on other people. This process lasts about a third of the years we lived on earth and makes us painfully aware of all our negative deeds and our shortcomings. This brings about a profound desire to compensate, which, of course, is only possible in a next incarnation.

After this, the soul enters the spiritual world under the guidance of the I AM, the unique self. Further experiences are gathered in the journey through the Hierarchies until the time has come to return to the earth. How the different sheaths (physical body, etheric body, and astral body) are fashioned will depend on what the soul has acquired in past lives.

What can fill us with amazement is that karma connects us with our parents, our brothers and sisters, our family, and with all of the friends and relations we have. Life experience shows that some encounters fill us with joy while others present us with considerable inner or outer challenges. In this light, a new way of considering autobiography is not to emphasize what we have done, but rather what we have become as a result of our interactions with other people. For example, the uncle who took us to our first concert, the elder brother who opened our eyes to great masters, a friend who introduced us to the philosophy of ancient India, have brought us great opportunities. When we reflect upon such events we find that our inner life has been much enhanced and that we become grateful for the ways in which we have been guided.

The word *karma* in Sanskrit means "compensation." In other words, we as human beings have to compensate, to put right, so to speak, our failures and misdeeds of previous incarnations. This cannot be achieved in one life; hence, a portion of our being, the I AM, reincarnates to correct in the course of time what he or she has done. Karma need not be looked upon as a penalty but as an opportunity to rectify the harm done to a relationship with another human being.

During our life on earth the individual needs many people. By and large with everybody we meet, we have a karmic connection. Something out of the past has brought us together now. What we do with the connection is largely up to the freedom of the individual. This is how necessity and freedom constantly intertwine; necessity comes out of the past, and freedom is pointing to the future. Everything depends on whether or not we are conscious of the nature of the relationship, which we can be with a certain maturity of soul. Some people pass one another by, totally unconscious of their inner connection. At other times we have an inkling that this other person has something to do with me, and I with him or her, but we turn away. In yet other cases, a man and a woman, for instance, might recognize that deep ties connect them and are able to bring this to consciousness for a fruitful life together.

When we speak of a love at first sight, we might note that in such cases the man or woman sees something *more* of the other. In other words, if the recognition is mutual, we are on the road to discovering something much more than the sexual attraction that may be present. Something of the soul and spirit of the other is revealed. We have actually beheld a supersensible part of one another. A loving couple has perceived something that others might not see. We know the expression, "I can't imagine what he sees in her" or "I can't imagine what she sees in him." The Dutch language has a rather appropriate saying that roughly translates: What two people feel for one another can hardly be judged by a third.

Death stands at the end of the way. The physical body returns to the elements through burial or cremation—ashes to ashes, dust to dust. The etheric body, however, severed from the physical, goes its way and disperses in the universe in the first three days after death. In time the astral body of passions, aspirations and desires will also spread out into the cosmos in kama loca. But the I AM, the unique, eternal being of our nature, will remain with us through eternity. It is in fact the only member that reincarnates—re-embodies, that is—and will seek to find an astral body, an etheric body, and a physical body in which it can return to the earth in accordance with its individual destiny. Rudolf Steiner remarks, strange as it might seem, that children choose their parents. The love of the child precedes the love of the parents who greet the child on earth.

We readily see that this mode of thinking, which is far from the materialistic concepts of our times, may not be easy to grasp at first. The more we reflect upon it, however, the more light it can throw on our manifold meetings and can make life a great deal more meaningful.

8

Karmic Relationships between Men and Women

In order to embark on this central theme, we must remember that within us we have both an eternal individuality, carried by the I AM or higher self, and a temporal personality, which we experience as our everyday self. The word "personality" has the Latin root *persona*, which means "mask." The mask hides the true face of the actor. If we reflect upon our nature, we find aspects of our personality that we experience as not particularly desirable. We may have a tendency to lie, lose our temper, be impatient, and so on. In addition to the shadow side of our personality, we can also discover a light realm. It includes all to which we aspire, all that in moments makes us kinder, more compassionate, more loving.

This tension in the human being, more widely acknowledged today than in the past, can bring about serious mental and emotional conditions, especially when we experience more the darkness and unresolved soul aspects than those of light and warmth. There is, however, a positive side to experiencing this tension. It can lead us to resolve to bring more light into our inner being. This can be achieved through prayer and meditation, through reading the Gospels, and by seeking to find the healing of the Christ in us. A meditation that can help us considerably in gaining the experience of the I AM or higher self, is the following. It was originally given in English by Mabel Collins, an English woman familiar with the spiritual world, whom Rudolf Steiner regarded very highly.

> More radiant than the Sun,
> Purer than snow,
> Finer than ether,
> Is the Self,
> The Spirit in my heart of hearts.
> I am this Self;
> This Self am I.

It is significant that the I AM is compared to the radiance of the sun (heavenly reality) and the purity of the snow (the winter covering the earth), and yet the I AM is more than either. It dwells in our "heart of hearts." This supersensible, eternal being incarnates like a ray of sunlight into our life between birth and death and excarnates for its journey through the Hierarchies and our post mortem existence. Before birth and after death we are surrounded by the Hierarchies in a way similar to our being embedded in the kingdoms of nature during earthly life.

The personality, our lower self, on the other hand, is formed by everything that is temporal, such as heredity, our surroundings, our education, and the circumstances of daily life. All this is not eternal and will pass.

One of the most powerful instinctive urges in the human being is sexual attraction. Individuals will vary as to how strong the urge is and to which extent it needs fulfillment. Sexuality without love, without affection for the partner, can turn into lust and sheer egoism, in which one is concerned only with the bare satisfaction of one's own passion. Such a situation can lead to great pain and soul anxiety for both partners.

As far as the I AM is concerned, we are neither man nor woman. Our gender is determined relatively late in the incarnation process on our way toward the earth through the guidance of the Hierarchies. Only during the latter stage, by the time the embryo is being formed, is gender determined. Yet, there is a difference between men and women.

Man	Human Being	Woman
I AM	I AM (eternal)	
	Astral	Astral
	Etheric	Etheric
Physical	Physical	

The above sketch attempts to clarify the difference. As far as our humanity is concerned, both sexes have a unique I AM, astral body, etheric body, and physical body. The sexuality is most apparent in the physical body of man and woman.

In a female incarnation there is a stronger astral and etheric body. This difference shows itself in woman's capacity for carrying a child. She can do so because her etheric body is strong enough. Her astral body is so constituted that she is more open to the influences of the spiritual world.

In a male incarnation the predominance lies in the relationship between the I AM and the physical body. The male incarnation is more directed toward the earth. Think of remarkable men who have constructed bridges, pierced tunnels through mountains (such as the Saint Gothard through the Alps), and accomplished remarkable engineering feats such as the development of aeronautics.

One might say that, on the whole, a man is more able to deal with matter and a woman is more intuitive and attuned toward relationships. In an ideal relationship, the qualities in a man and a woman complement one another. Of course, increasingly in the world today, there are women bridge builders and men notable for their intuition. This is as it should be, as the personality more and more freely explores who it is and what its destiny may be. It can make choices that override the nature of its bodies. Each must discover for himself or herself whether the choices made in life are destiny-fulfilling or not.

The great Brancacci chapel fresco by Masaccio (1401–1427?) in the church of Santa Maria del Carmine, Florence, Italy, depicts in a most dramatic manner the Expulsion from Paradise. Both Adam and Eve are naked. Adam covers his face in shame and turns his head towards the earth, whereas Eve turns her painful countenance toward the heavens and covers her breasts with the right hand, and her sexual organs with the left. Through this great work of art, we see the soul of man turned toward the earth and that of the woman toward the heavens.

Love blossoms in the soul and spiritual spheres, although it may be rooted in a strong sexuality. The joy of being together and sharing interests can lead to happiness and contentment. In such a case, sexuality is the manifestation of the soul connection that exists between the partners. A loving relationship can certainly include a healthy sexuality, but in such a case affection, caring for the other, will also play a fundamental role.

A moment's reflection will reveal to us that falling in love (or rising in love as it was characterized earlier) belongs to one of the great mysteries of life. Falling in love can happen at any stage in life, quite unexpectedly, as if at random or by chance, through the eyes, the smile, a gesture, the voice, and touch. There is usually an element of surprise and anticipation connected with the encounter. It lifts us out of the ordinary and can change our whole attitude. It can move us most deeply with gratitude and happiness and at the same time quicken the soul with many profound questions. Why has this happened to us? What can be the significance of this sudden incision in our destiny? As the relationship develops, sharing biographies and life experiences, we touch upon the compatibility between us. What do we really share? What interests do we have in common? How can we help one another to grow, to become more interested in the world, to feel that we can assist others through the love that we experience for one another? It is not surprising that in Roman and Greek mythology Cupid (Eros) is depicted as a mischievous, blindfolded demigod, who shot his arrows indiscriminately through the hearts of innocent youths and young maidens so that they fell deeply in love. This may be why we say that love is blind. Cupid's activity was a random one and he delighted in the results of his pranks.

If the concept of karma (in other words, destiny) is envisaged, a new light can be thrown on the significance of relationships. During our life on earth we meet many people who may well have played a part in our life in a previous incarnation. We now meet them again in joy or sorrow in order to continue or compensate for a previous life situation, which may or may not have been harmonious. Recognizing the former connection in this life may be obscured, because the conditions of a common previous incarnation were completely different. Our gender may be different, our surroundings and language are likely not the same, and our individual station in life may not be comparable with the one we held in the past. So, when we meet again in this life, our mutual recognition may take time to awaken. On the other hand, sometimes we feel deeply connected with another right away, although we might not know why.

If we think about our relationships in this light, a confidence can grow in the soul that there is a deeper meaning to our encounters than merely coincidence. In fact, it strengthens our soul life if we can develop an attitude of wonder in relation to the people we meet and ask ourselves What lesson can I learn from this person? This attitude will enrich our inner life, although it will not necessarily lift the veil completely on the mystery of love.

9

The Sevenfold Ladder of Love and the Double

To consider love from the seven aspects of the human being can throw further light on the mystery. These seven levels of love interweave in the human being. Only for the sake of clarity do we divide them into a ladder from the sensuous, instinctive, profane, to the nobler and sacred forms.

We shall consider love as it is connected with each of the members of the human being:

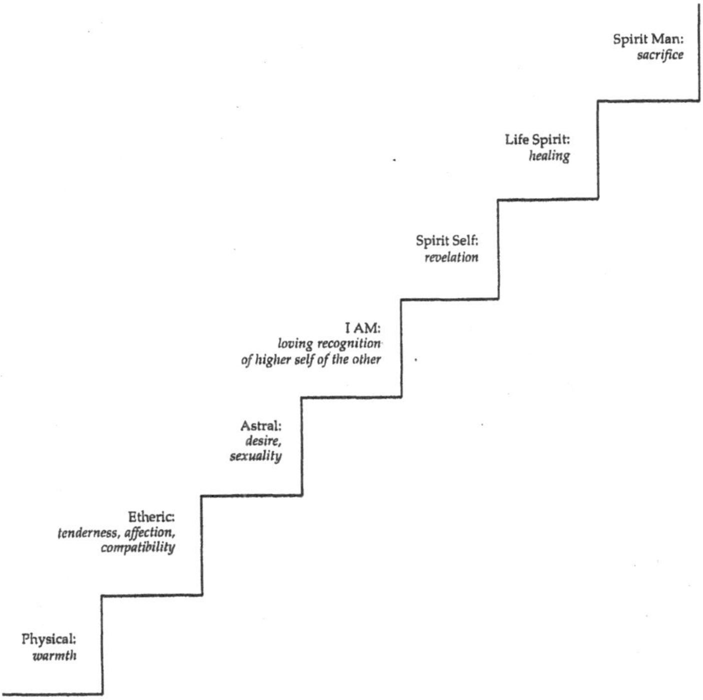

Love at the level of the physical body expresses itself in warmth—the warmth of the baby on its mother's breast, the warmth of the young child who cuddles in bed with its parents. The first stage is essentially non-sexual, pertaining to the development of the child from birth to the change of teeth.

The love at the level of the etheric body manifests itself as affection, tenderness, compatibility in everyday life, and respect for the other. This is born in the human being between the change of teeth and puberty and develops later in adulthood.

At the level of love of the astral body, love between man and woman expresses itself as desire. It permeates the warmth of physical togetherness, tenderness and affection. It is at this level that the procreative possibility arises. The astrality in the young person unfolds from puberty onward, and it is at this stage that the attraction between the sexes becomes a strongly-present factor.

At the level of the I AM, love awakens with the sense of *recognition*. The loving one recognizes an aspect of the higher self in the other that resides beyond the mere outer appearance. It is particularly at this level of the "I am" recognition that a karmic element plays a role. The recognition often has its source in a previous embodiment. We know quite suddenly, consciously or unconsciously, that we have been together and that in this life we are called upon to continue a connection from the past. The nature of the connection in this life might not reveal itself immediately; it can take years, but it has arisen out of the loving relationship beyond this life. It is commonly expressed as "I feel I've always known you."

Love in the sentient soul expresses itself in strong passionate feelings without much objectivity. In the heart and mind soul, love manifests itself as more analytical: Can I have confidence in the other? How can I overcome my doubt in this relationship? In the consciousness soul love expresses itself in a more objective manner; though warm, it leaves both parties free, based on mutual confidence and respect.

The three higher levels of the human being are by no means fully developed; in fact, we can only, at the present stage of our development, have an inkling of them. But something in the realm of true love carried also in the spirit can give us an idea of how it could blossom.

Love at the level of the spirit self expresses itself as revelation. What is meant here, for instance, is that when we travel with a loved one—let's say to Egypt, Greece, Turkey, Israel, India, or Japan—certain happenings may conjure forth experiences of a former life together. We realize that we would not have had this revelation without the other. At our present stage of consciousness, however, we rarely attain an all-embracing awareness of such experiences.

Love at the stage of life spirit manifests itself as healing love. One who loves out of this level is a healing presence for family, friends, and community. Partners who love at this level not only feel a greater sense of well-being in each other's presence, but their relationship is healing for the community in which they live.

We can have only an inkling of love at the highest spiritual level, which will manifest itself in the distant future. Love related to spirit man becomes apparent in sacrifice. In the words of the New Testament, "Blessed is he who lays down his life for another." Its highest expression lives in Christ Jesus offering his life for humanity.

In our younger years the sensual part of love may play a prominent part, and as a relationship develops in a fruitful and harmonious way, the higher and the more spiritual aspects tend to come to expression. One can clearly see in a biography of two people who are deeply connected whether or not something of the loftier aspects fills their lives.

Unfortunately, today's relationships between men and women are fraught with difficulties. Women want to be recognized as individuals; men struggle with their feelings. Formerly clear roles become confused as new possibilities emerge. The role of sex in a relationship is increasingly troublesome as the strictures of church and tradition come into question for some, and men and women at early ages find themselves making difficult decisions on their own. Bringing sex too early into a relationship can delay or even prevent two souls from truly getting to know one another. Contraception, which allows couples to make choices about pregnancy, also may weaken a sense of responsibility and commitment to the depth of the deeds being performed. In one sense, karma is being interfered with, and the intentions of the spiritual world may be blocked or deviated.

Sexual promiscuity, hardly a term in use anymore, gives the illusion of liberating us, though all the while it may be misleading us into taking relationships for granted or using instead of recognizing one another. Our instinct can lead us to change partners frequently. The nobler aspects of relationships can be karmicly obscured; partners don't recognize one another in their real being. Attraction rather than love rises like a straw-fire and lacks the strength required for living together through joys and sorrows. Relationships may remain superficial and fail to attain maturity through time. The initial meeting may certainly be karmic, but it is only in the course of time that a certain fulfillment of the relationship can be achieved. Modern western civilization tends to rob us of a gradual maturing in our relationships. Everything points to an immediate fulfillment of our wishes and desires. If goodwill is present, love between man and woman is the greatest schooling of life enabling both souls to ripen.

The shadow side of the seven aspects of love: The working of the double

What is meant by the double? It is that part of our being that contains every facet of our soul that still lives in darkness, ignored, rejected, unseen. It is a shadow side that everyone carries. It represents not only the results of misdeeds and shortcomings of our present incarnation, but also the unredeemed aspects of former lives.

In the past, human beings were protected from their double through the guidance and conventions of the church. These protective forces have largely disappeared, and human beings have to find their own way in life, often with overwhelming, conflicting, and confusing directives from others who set themselves up as authorities.

In the literature of the last two centuries, aspects of the double have been clearly expressed. For instance, in the poem "La Nuit de Décembre (December night)" by Alfred de Musset (1810–1857), the speaker experiences his double as he sits by the deathbed of his father. In the poems of Charles Baudelaire (1821–1867), *Les Fleurs du Mal* (Flowers of evil), in *The Strange Case of Dr. Jekyll and Mr Hyde* by Robert Louis Stevenson (1850–1894), in Oscar Wilde's (1854–1900) *The Picture of Dorian Gray*, and in the poignant works of Fyodor M. Dostoyevski (1821–1881), the double is recognized.

We experience the double under certain stressful conditions as a being who resembles ourselves, though we see it as disfigured, ugly, and often frightening. In a relationship that may have started in a loving, harmonious way, it can happen that instead of seeing the positive, luminous side of the other, we perceive the darker aspects of our partner. The honeymoon is over. The raw reality of everyday life rears up and destroys the joy that previously reigned; nasty arguments ensue, ugly words are exchanged, and the whole atmosphere in the house can become tense. If it happens in front of children, they are often deeply affected by these quarrels. It is obviously not the better part of either partner that comes to expression at such moments.

We can establish also the sevenfold ladder of the shadow side of relationships. At the physical level the connection becomes cold, distant. At the level of the etheric body, there is indifference, a lack of affection, compatibility and respect. At the level of the astral body there is either aversion, often accompanied by vocal and physical abuse, or an excessive, lustful sexual desire aimed at satisfying one's own physical needs. At the level of the I AM, a blindness toward the other develops; the ideal in the relationship is shattered. At the level of spirit self, the revelation ceases and boredom in each other's company sets in. At the level of life spirit, rather than healing, the partners make one another sick, sometimes literally; they can't bear to be in one another's presence any longer. At the level of "Spirit Man" the shadow side is experienced as the grossest selfishness and egoism. There is no giving, and taking consumes the soul.

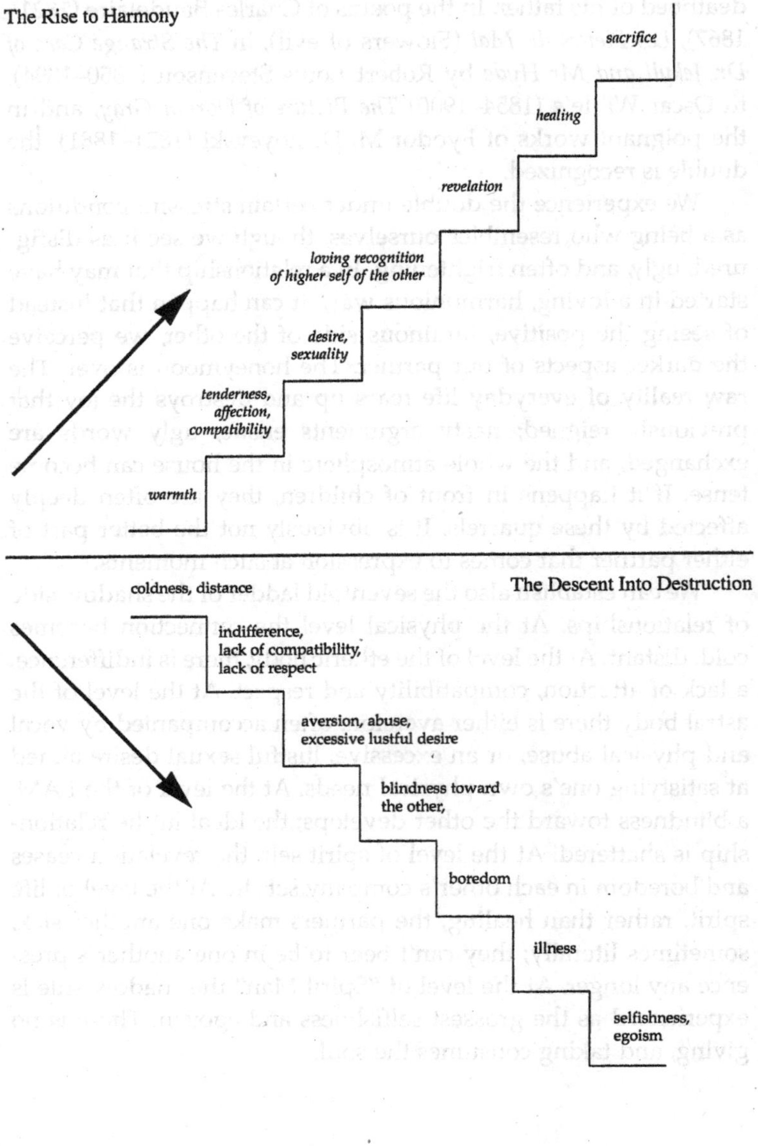
The Rise to Harmony
sacrifice
healing
revelation
loving recognition of higher self of the other
desire, sexuality
tenderness, affection, compatibility
warmth
coldness, distance
The Descent Into Destruction
indifference, lack of compatibility, lack of respect
aversion, abuse, excessive lustful desire
blindness toward the other,
boredom
illness
selfishness, egoism

The negative side may take over most easily when there is stress, not only with one another, but with the children, or when money matters are difficult. Everything now depends on the inner strength of the partners concerned whether a reconciliation, a new start, is possible. Can the two dissipate the clouds that hang over the relationship? Can something of the original, joyful aspects of the relationship be renewed? This requires a great deal of inner work: sacrifice, forgiveness, and a wish to understand. Unfortunately, in many marriages, difficulties lead to separation. The partners may not be awake enough to face the karmic task that brought them together in the first place. When we understand that karma and destiny are involved in our relationships, new levels of wisdom and resolve can be ours to heal what has gone awry and become a healing presence in our families and in the communities in which we work and live.

10

Rudolf Steiner's View of Love

Throughout his books and lectures, Rudolf Steiner brings light to the mystery of love. I am grateful to Richard Lewis who has collected quotations on this theme from Rudolf Steiner's work into three volumes entitled *Love, Marriage and Sex in the Light of Spiritual Science*. The earliest reference is found at the end of the first chapter in *The Philosophy of Spiritual Activity* written in 1894:

> Pity enters my heart when the mental picture of a person who arouses pity appears in my consciousness. The way to the heart is through the head. Love is no exception.

We read in this text that love is not merely a feeling but arises in the human soul because thinking, the forming of mental pictures, is centrally involved. In simple language, we find that when we love someone, we also think about that person. In fact, if love were only a feeling, it would be fleeting and have no value in time; it would be an emotional response that could never be deepened. The above quotation by Rudolf Steiner makes this very clear. Moreover, implicit in the text is the suggestion that love has stages of development, from that which is more sensual— connected, for instance, with our physical instincts—to higher, more idealistic levels. Love can grow.

It is interesting to note that Shakespeare, in *The Merchant of Venice*, questions whether the head or the heart is the source of love.

> Tell me where is fancy [love] bred
> Or in the heart or in the head?
> How begot how nourished?
> Reply, reply
> It is engendered in the eyes
> With gazing fed...
>
> Act III, scene ii

In this song Shakespeare refers to love arising out of seeing; love is not blind. Steiner elaborates on this seeing in the following way:

> Whenever [love] is not merely the expression of bare sexual instinct, it depends on the mental picture we form of the loved one. And the more idealistic these mental pictures are, just so much the more blessed is our love. Here, too, thought is the father of feeling. It is said that love makes us blind to the failings of the loved one. But this can be expressed the other way round, namely, that it is just for the good qualities that love opens the eyes. Many pass by these good qualities without noticing them. One, however, perceives them, and just because he does, love awakens in the soul. What else has he done but made a mental picture of what hundreds have failed to see? Love is not theirs, because they lack the mental picture.
>
> *Philosophy of Freedom*
> translated by Michael Wilson

We can ask the question, What is the difference between a selfish feeling of love and one that is unselfish? If we have expectations that the other gratify our desires and meet our needs, our love is selfish. We don't leave the loved one free to be whoever they are and do whatever they choose. If, however, we create a space in our heart for the loved one, the quality of that love will be unselfish, for it is ready to receive the other as they are, without placing all kinds of restrictions on them. The progress we can make from the more selfish kind of love to the more selfless can be an ennobling transformation but one fraught with difficulties, especially in our time.

In "Threshold of the Spiritual World," Rudolf Steiner expresses in a most beautiful and sensitive manner the genuine nature of love:

> Love is an experience of the other in one's own soul. To experience love, however, a sort of veil must be drawn

in the soul over the self-feeling or "I"-experience present in its depths. Then, because its own powers are muted, the joys and sorrows of the other arise in the soul. In this way, love, which is the source of the most genuine moral impulse in human life, germinates.

Love is for us the most important fruit of human experience in the sensory world. If you penetrate the nature of love, or compassion, you will discover how the spiritual expresses its truth in the sensory world.

Genuine love and true kindness of the soul are experiences that strengthen consciousness, giving it the forces it needs to enter into clairvoyance. I said that we must prepare the soul before it can have suprasensory experiences. It must be added that a genuine capacity for love and a desire for true human kindness, compassion, and empathy are among the many means of such preparation.

An excessive "I"-feeling in the physical world works against morality.

To develop a genuinely moral attitude in our souls, we must mute the "I"-feeling with tendencies to compassion and love.

"Threshold of the Spiritual World"
part I of *A Way of Self-Knowledge*
translated by Christopher Bamford

One might say that there is an inherent paradox, because on the one hand we have to develop an I-strength in the world, and yet in order to love we have to mute our own powers, throw a veil over them, in a sense, to experience the other in our soul. In grasping this concept, we must remain aware that the way to selflessness is a path, and so it may begin in selfishness. Thus, we can accept that this child of ours—or this child who we were!—may act in ways that are quite selfish. Yet this selfishness can be a rich loam out of which the selflessness of an I-consciousness can arise. Its roots push against the soil and rocks of selfishness and in doing so gain strength. In the course of life— depending, of course, on the character of the person and the good fortune of his relationships and experiences—an unselfishness emerges that bears the rich fruits of love. This development of selflessness is reflected by Rudolf Steiner in the following verse on the spirit of Michael:

> Victorious Spirit
> Flame through the impotence of irresolute souls.
> Burn out the egoism,
> Ignite the compassion
> That selflessness, the life stream of mankind,
> Wells up as a source of spirit rebirth.

In the fifth lecture of *The Folk Souls and their Mission,* Rudolf Steiner highlights how the human being can gain a new relationship to love, to humanity and to the purpose of earth evolution. At first Steiner discusses the importance of the equilateral triangle in the occult stream of mankind, its origin found in the ancient Egyptian mysteries. This mystery is hinted at today on the U.S. one-dollar bill, where we find a pyramid with the equilateral triangle above it, an eye in its center. This eye is the all-seeing eye of God, which in the human being becomes insight, or wisdom. Steiner then brings an imagination of love arising at the center of the equilateral triangle. This imagination represents a perfect harmony among thinking, feeling, and willing. Steiner discusses such a harmony many times in his lectures, especially when he speaks about the first three of the six subsidiary exercises: control of thinking, determination of the will, balance in feeling (in *Guidance to Esoteric Training, How to Know Higher Worlds,* and *An Outline of Esotric Science*).

> Man is called upon first of all to bring about an equilibrium between thought, feeling and will within himself, by means of which he can from within radiate and carry over on to the earth what this equilibrium between thought, feeling and will signifies. . . .

> In occult symbolism this mission of the earth has always been expressed in quite a special way by means of a geometrical figure. If you go through all geometrical figures, you will find none, which so exactly corresponds to the balance of the three activities as the equilateral triangle. If you merely draw it, you will find the three sides equal, the three angles equal, each angle is equidistant from the others and all are equidistant from the center. The center of the equilateral triangle is an absolute symbol of a balance of forces. . . . The deeds of the "I" in man signify nothing else than the creating of an active center in his nature, whereby this state of equilibrium can be prepared from within.
>
> The secret of this mission [of the earth] is expressed in the fact that through this cooperation, through this equilibrium of the three forces, the inner being actually produces something new. A fourth element is thus really added to the three preceding ones, and this fourth is the element of love. Love can only develop in the world when an absolute equilibrium comes about between the three forces.
>
> Thus our planet is the planet of Love, and therefore this equilibrium which, so to speak, is established in the cooperation of these three forces, produces as an effect the "activity of Love", and this is to be woven into the whole of evolution.

Rudolf Steiner gave one of his books the title *An Outline of Esoteric Science*—an outline. In spite of its depths and breadth this work presents only an overview. If one reads it attentively, one finds that several sentences at the end summarize the essence of this basic work.

> The Wisdom of the outer world [of past ages] becomes inner Wisdom—Wisdom in man himself. And when thus resurrected in the inner life, in the I [am] of [the human

being], it grows into the seed of Love. Wisdom is the premise, the forerunner of Love; Love is the outcome of Wisdom re-born in the I [am] of [the human being]."

translated by George Adams

For those readers who wish to deepen their connection with Rudolf Steiner's insights, an appendix has been included with quotations from various works relevant to our theme.

11

The Lord of Love in the Gospels

Throughout Christendom from the earliest times we find representations in churches and cathedrals of Christ amid the four apocalyptic figures. The four evangelists are traditionally connected each with one of these beings.

Luke *Bull*	*Lion*	Mark
	Christ	
Matthew *Human Being*		John *Eagle*

St. Matthew is connected with the figure of the human being. His Gospel is the longest and most detailed account of the life of Christ Jesus. St. Matthew can be characterized as the historian who at great length, quoting from the Old Testament, shows that the insights of the prophets have been fulfilled in the life of Christ Jesus. He opens with a narration on the birth of Jesus in Bethlehem. He addressed his Gospel essentially to the Jews.

St. Mark is represented by the symbol of the lion. His Gospel is the most concise of the four and in its way carries a sense of forceful urgency, often using such words as "now," "then," and "immediately." It contains no childhood story, and Christ appears in it forcefully as the supreme, white magician. St. Mark's is characterized as the most dramatic of the Gospels. It was addressed to the Romans who had to learn to give up ancient mystery practices so that they could receive the new message brought into the world by Christ.

The tone and quality in the Gospel of St. Luke is very different from the others. St. Luke is known by the symbol of the bull, which signifies the will transformed into healing forces. We know that St. Luke himself was a painter and a healer, deeply conversant with the medical arts of his time. In addition to telling the story of the childhood of the Jesus child, this Gospel contains some nineteen parables. The Gospel mainly focuses on scenes of prayer and healing; for example, in the story of the Prodigal Son and of the Good Samaritan. It has been described as the Christianized Buddha Gospel of compassion. This connection can be glimpsed in its structure; its three times eight chapters reflect the eight-fold path.

The Gospel of St. John has been regarded as the most profound and also the most esoteric of the four Gospels. St. John is symbolized by the eagle, which is the transformation of the scorpion (death) into the soaring eagle (resurrected life). St. John wrote his Gospel as a very old man, when he was over one hundred years of age. One can feel throughout this profound, meditative work the inspiration not only of Christ, but also of Mary the Mother, with whom St. John spent many years in Ephesus. Mary lived in a little house on top of one of the hills overlooking Ephesus, whereas John mostly dwelt by the seashore, close to where the glorious temple to Diana had been built in earlier times. The ancient Ephesian practices were devoted to the mysteries of the word. We know that Plato was initiated in the last glow of the rituals surrounding the goddess Diana. It should be noted that during his exile on Patmos, St. John wrote the Apocalypse before he wrote the Gospel.

While the first three Gospels are profound accounts of Christ Jesus and show Him to be the fulfillment of the prophecies, the Lord of power and healing, it is in the Gospel of St. John that Christ Jesus most emerges as the Lord of Love. In the middle of his Gospel, John reveals his initiation by Christ and from thereon refers to himself as the "disciple whom the Lord loved." The great blessing he received became central to the rest of his life. The story is told in The Golden Legend that when John was near the end of his life, barely able to walk anymore, he was carried back and forth to the church by his own followers. At every pause for rest along the way, he repeated the same words: "Little children, love ye one another." One day the followers, wondering at this, asked why he repeated the same phrase again and again. "It is the commandment of the Lord," he replied, "and if it alone is followed, it is enough." It is interesting to note that the Gospel of St. John does not speak of the childhood of Jesus of Nazareth, but instead at its very opening relates in exalted words the emergence of the Logos (i.e. the Word, or Christ) in the evolution of humanity: "In the beginning was the Word, and the Word was with God, and the Word was a Divine Being. He was in the very beginning with God."

The Gospel of John is clearly divided into two parts. The first ten chapters relate the ministry and the miracles performed by Christ Jesus. The eleventh chapter relates the initiation of John Lazarus and the final ten chapters are devoted to the events from Palm Sunday through Holy Week, culminating in the death and resurrection of Christ. John was the only disciple present at the foot of the cross with Mary the Mother and Mary Magdalene. The other disciples had fled. He also received one of the seven last words from the cross: "Woman, see, that is your son. See, that is your mother." And from that time onwards, John kept Mary by his side.

In what follows, I am indebted to the work of Rudolf Frieling, *Agape—die Goettliche Liebe im Johannes Evangelium* (Stuttgart: Verlag Urachhaus).

One of the characteristics of the John Gospel is that the word "love" (in the sense of *agape,* spiritual love) is found 48 times. It should be noted, and we have discussed this earlier, that apart from several exceptions, in John's Gospel Christ always exclusively speaks about the noblest, heavenly love, the Greek *agape. Philia,* the love of friendship (which we have in the city of Philadelphia—the city of brotherly love), is rarely used in the John Gospel. The word *eros* is not used at all by the Christ.

There are three forms of *agape* in the John Gospel: the *agape* of the Father, the *agape* of the Son, and the *agape* of the disciples. An example of the first category, *agape* of the Father, is in John 3: 16 where it is described that God has loved the world to whom he gave his only Son: "The Father showed his love for the world through this, that he offered up his only Son. From now on, no one shall perish who fills himself with his power; indeed, he shall win a share of the life that is beyond time."

The *agape* of the Father is also seen in John 10:17-18 where it is written, "That is why the Father loves me, because I lay down my life, that I may take it up anew. No one can take my life from me; but in full freedom I myself offer it up. I have the power to give it away, and also the power to receive it anew."

> John 14:21 reads: "Whoever knows my aims and takes them into his will, he it is who truly loves me. And he who loves me will be loved by my Father, and I will love him and reveal myself to him."

> As a fourth example we can look at John 15:9–10: "As the Father has loved me, so I have loved you—live on in my love. If you take my aims into your will, then you will live on in my love, just as I have taken the aims of my Father into my will and live on in HIS love."

> Also in John 16:25: "For the Father himself loves you because you have loved me and have believed that I come from the Father."

In each of these instances, the word *agape* is the one used. Again, the word appears in passage after passage about Christ Jesus and his love. In John 11:5 we read, "Jesus loved Martha and her sister and Lazarus." At the beginning of the washing of the feet before the feast in John 13:1, we read, "He loved all those who had become his own from out of mankind, and he sustained this love to its fulfillment."

We have a mention of the beloved disciple in John 13:23: "Now one of his disciples was at the table, lying close to the breast of Jesus, the disciple whom Jesus loved." A very important passage on the words of Christ is given in John 15:12 and 13: "This is the task I put before you, that you love on another as I have loved you. No man can have greater love than this, that he offer up his life for his friends." And as a final reference, we can point to John 15:17 where the Christ says, "This I say to you out of the fullness of my power—love one another."

> Finally, in the Gospel of John we hear Christ Jesus telling his disciples again and again to love one another, to love in the sense of agape:
>
> John 13:34-35: "A new task and aim I give you: Love one another! As I have loved you, so you should love one another. By this everyone shall recognize you as my disciples, that you have love for one another."
>
> John 15:12-13: "This is the task I put before you, that you love on another as I have loved you. No man can have greater love than this, that he offer up his life for his friends."
>
> John 14:15: "If you truly love me you will take my aims into your will."
>
> John 14:21: "Whoever knows my aims and takes them into his will, he it is who truly loves me. And he who loves me will be loved by my Father, and I will love him and reveal myself to him."
>
> John 14:23: "Jesus answered, 'Whoever truly loves me bears my word in himself, and my Father will love him, and we [the disciples] will come to him and dwell with him for ever.'"

John 14:28: "You have heard that I said: I go away, and yet I come to you. If you really loved me you would rejoice that I go to the Father, for the Father is greater than I."

It is noteworthy that most of the passages about love in the John Gospel are found after the raising of Lazarus in Chapter 11. These are the chapters in which St. John records the passion of Christ during Holy Week, which begins with the Palm Sunday. It is also important to realize that all of the *agape* quotations are spoken to the disciples in a most intimate setting, after the Last Supper on the evening of Maundy Thursday.

When we reflect upon the quotations above, we find that they are sentences for meditation that can greatly deepen our understanding of the Mystery of Christ as the Lord of Love. Many men and women through the ages have taken up a devotional study of this Gospel in particular for the fostering of their spiritual life. If read with devotion and understanding, the Gospel of St. John is enormously rewarding. It in itself can become for the sincere seeker a schooling in the mysteries of love.

12

Some Thoughts on Sacred and Profane Love

Paintings that I have come to know intimately over the years I also find intimately connected with the theme of love. Titian (1490–1576), the Venetian painter who is first rank among artists of the Renaissance, painted many beautiful nudes, and the one that appears in his work titled "Sacred and Profane Love" is perhaps among his most enchanting. The picture shows two women seated at what appears to be a rectangular marble water fount decorated with an elaborately carved frieze. On the far side of the fount, a small child leans, looking into the waters.

The two women are beautiful. With the title in mind, we could say they represent two contrasting Venuses. The richly dressed and bejeweled woman to the left with a delicate crown of leaves on her head is Venus Naturalis. The equally beautiful, naked woman on the right represents the Divine or Celestial Venus. The cherubic child who stands behind the fount and between the two women dips his right hand into the water. He may well be Cupid, who confirms for the viewer that this picture is about love.

The naked Venus is demure in her bearing. She wears a loose scarf over her lap. In her left hand she carries aloft a dark object, a small, votive lamp. It is lit with the flame of Divine Love and is the representative of the eternal feminine. This Venus is not distracted by worldly possessions. Venus Naturalis in her voluminous gown, on the other hand, reminds us that earthly love is fettered by the wealth of this world. Further, we notice that there is a remarkable resemblance between the two women. In this way it may be suggested that something of celestial love is reflected in the earthly counterpart. We see that while the earthly one seems as yet unaware of her heavenly sister, the Divine Venus looks lovingly at her earthly reflection.

Let us turn now to another master in the realm of art, the great Dutch painter, Rembrandt Harmenszoon van Rijn (1606–1669). Among his many magnificent paintings, I turn to one completed a year before his death. It is known as "The Married Couple" or "Husband and Wife." [perhaps "The Jewish Bride"] We do not know the precise identity of the characters, but the man appears to hold his wife with deep tenderness. The rich, golden cape worn by the man is beautifully draped over his right arm. His right hand rests upon the woman's heart, and his left hand is placed in a protective gesture on her left shoulder. She responds with affection by placing one hand on his as a confirmation of their union. Her right hand rests modestly on the lap of her red dress. Their conjugal love is expressed to perfection in the flow of the gold and the red. The painting could represent the actual moment of betrothal.

Leonardo da Vinci (1452–1519) painted his famous fresco, the Last Supper, in Santa Maria della Grazie in Milan, Italy. While making his preparations for the painting, Leonardo made a most impressive sketch of the head of Christ Jesus. This is one of the most remarkable portraits of Christ Jesus. With its slightly bent head and downcast eyes, it reflects the depth and devotion of this great being's nature. As a contrast we have a late portrait of the Christ by Rembrandt that in its simplicity speaks more of Christ Jesus in his dedication as a healer of mankind.

Perhaps the profoundest expression of the nature of Love is found in an epistle by Saint Paul in Corinthians I, 13:4-7:

> Love makes the soul great
> Love fills the soul with healing goodness
> Love does not know envy,
> It knows no boasting,
> It does not allow of falseness,
> Love does not harm that which is decent,
> It drives out self-seeking,
> Love does not allow the inner balance to be lost,
> It does not bear a grudge,
> It does not rejoice over injustice,

It rejoices only in the truth.
Love bears all things,
Is always prepared to have faithful trust,
It may hope for everything and is all-patient.

It is commonly known that St. Paul addressed his epistles to particular communities in order to help them understand the being of and the new reality brought by Christ. In that time Corinth was known across the whole of the Mediterranean as a city of cultural dissipation and sexual aberrations. St. Paul attempted to correct the prevalent excesses of profane love by drawing the attention of the first Christian congregation in Corinth to the deeper aspects of sacred love.

It is a cherished hope, which many share, that in the course of time the human being will evermore gradually transform profane love into its sacred counterpart and learn to recognize the Christ-light and love in every individual.

All translations of the New Testament are taken from *The New Testament, A rendering by Jon Madsen* published by Floris Books in 1994.

Appendix

This Appendix contains further quotations by Rudolf Steiner (with kind permission from Richard Lewis) including crucial passages on the theme of love. Richard Lewis has made his own translation of these passages; therefore, the wording will differ from that in published versions by other translators. Titles of references given sometimes refer to books published in English, sometimes to individual lectures that may be part of a collection published under another title, and sometimes to material that has not been published in English.

From "Theosophy in Relation to John's Gospel," October 31, 1906, Munich:

The sentence is true which says, 'Whoever does not leave father and mother and brothers for my sake, he cannot be my disciple.' That means, whoever does not forget the old principles of the tribe and carry over love from the bloodlines to all human beings, he cannot be a follower of Christ. The old tribal gods had undertaken indivisible marriages with their tribes; they had to pass away, with their tribes.

From "The Origin of Evil," November 22, 1906, Berlin:

Love appears to begin with as sex-love and evolves up to the highest divine love. But all love, lower and higher, is breath of the gods...But Lucifer brought love into connection with the self, and self-love was added to self-consciousness. That was beautifully expressed in the Paradise story, 'and they saw that they were naked.' That means that human beings saw themselves for the first time; previously they had seen only the surrounding world. They had only an earth-consciousness but not a self-consciousness.

From *Theosophy of the Rosicrucian*, May 27, 1907, Munich:

The question can arise: is there a relationship between mother and child, which is permanent? Yes, there is such a thing. Much more intimate, much more firmly than any relationship that can be spun out here on earth. Mother-love, at first, has an animalistic character; it is a kind of natural instinct. When the child is growing up, then this relationship fashions itself into a moral, and ethical, a spiritual one. When mother and child learn to think in common, have shared feelings, then the natural instinct recedes; it only provided the opportunity, that the beautiful bond should be interwoven that comprises within itself mother-love and child—in the very highest sense. What then develops as mutual understanding, as intimate love, that maintain its continuity up into the spiritual worlds, even when one of them seems to be separated for a certain time, because the one dies before and the other one is left behind. After this period of time, the bond that is interwoven here is just as vitally stimulating and intimate; they are together, but all animalistic purely natural instincts first are gotten rid of. What interweaves as soulful feelings, soulful thoughts from one being to another here on earth, up there is not hindered through the limitations that are present here. . . .
What happens here through love, through friendship, through intimate understanding between people, they are building blocks which build temples up there in the spirit realm, and for the man who is penetrated by this certainty, it must be an elevated feeling to know that when here already bonds are interwoven from soul to soul, this is the foundation of an eternal becoming.

From *Theosophy of the Rosicrucian*, June 5, 1907, Munich:

The most beautiful, selfless love consists in this, which one does not need the other that one can also get along without him. The human being then loves not because of himself, but because of the other one. He also then does not lose anything, if he is left alone by the other one. For this is, to be sure, necessary that one can have insight into the value of a human being, and one can only learn that, in that one becomes involved into the world.

From *Christ and Love,* March 24, 1908, Berlin:

So that love could be developed on earth, the body had to be developed at first on a primitive level. Love had to be instigated in the lowest form as sexual love so as to develop itself up through the various stages, and in the end, when the earth has arrived at its completion in its last epoch, love ennobled will be elevated to pure spiritual love.

From *The Principle of Spiritual Economy,* April 6, 1908, Malsch:

No longer can one say it is suffering to be separated from what one loves. For the Christ power will lead us together with everything that we want to love from soul to soul. The Christ power will make the ties between what loves one another. The suffering that could come, thereby that one is separated from what one loves—through the Christ power this separation will be overcome.

From *The Principle of Spiritual Economy,* June 11, 1909, Budapest::

The saying of Christ: 'Whoever does not leave father and mother cannot be my disciple,' is to be so understood that the blood-love is to be transformed into brother love, which comprises all human beings with equal power. Spiritual science does not wish to take away anything from all these sayings of the Bible, but it can only join to them a deeper understanding of the Christian grace, if it is only accepted in the proper sense. The power of spiritual love is what Christ first brought to the human soul at His appearance upon earth. And with the blood that flowed out of the wounds of the savior upon Golgotha, so to speak, the superfluous surplus blood of humanity was sacrificed; through this deed, the doctrine was sealed that states: the individual has to stand by the individual, the human brother to the human brother.

From *The Gospel of St. John,* May 20, 1908 Hamburg:

Let us ask: 'What then is essential for love? What is essential in order that one person love another?' It is this: that he be in possession of his full self-consciousness, that he be wholly independent. No one can love another in the full sense of the word, if this love is not a free gift of one person to the other. My hand does not love my organism; only one who is independent, one who is not bound to the other person, can love him. To this end the human being had to become an ego being. The ego had to be implanted in the threefold human body, so the earth might, through mankind, fulfill its mission of love. Therefore, you will understand esoteric Christianity when it streamed down from divine beings . . . now love streams into the earth and the bearer of love can only be the independent ego, which develops by degrees in the course of the evolution of the earth.

From *The Apocalypse* June 24, 1908, Nuremberg:

The forces, which brought men together, were forces, which had their material foundation in the blood. If men had simply been placed side by side in their present form, that which was to develop in humanity would never have been originated. ... It is the mission of our earth to bring men together in love. In the future, when the seventh trumpet has sounded and the earth has dissolved, when it has lost its physical substantiality and is changed into a heavenly astral body, the love, the force of love will have flowed into the whole human race, into everything earthly. For this power of love must flow-in as the earth mission of humanity.

From "Love and its Meaning in the World", December 17, 1912, Zurich:

Love of wisdom is not egotistic, for this love becomes ever greater the more we approach death; it grows to the same extent as the prospect of gaining something from our wisdom becomes smaller.

If we grasp the law of reincarnation, then we know the significance of love in the world in detail and in the totality.

Deeds of love are those deeds, which from the very beginning do not seek their reward in the life to come.

Everything that we do out of the impulse of love reveals itself to be such that through it we are repaying debts.

The sole actions from which we gain nothing in the future are those that we do in genuine, true love. In their subconsciousness all men know this; therefore they do deeds of love so sparingly.

A soul must be far progressed in its development if it takes pleasure in doing deeds of love, from which it gains nothing for itself.

We gain nothing to satisfy our egotism from deeds of love, but the world gains so much the more.

Occultism says: love is the same for the world, as the sun is for outer life.

It is wisdom to sow as much love as possible upon earth.

Interest for the earth's development is the spiritual matrix for love of the world; a spiritual science without love would be a danger for humanity. We should not sermonize on love, but it should and shall come into the world, this love, in that we spread real spiritual knowledge about things.

When we exercise love, nurture love, then creative forces are released into the world.

We owe our existence to deeds of love from the past. As strong as we are for this reason, so strongly are we indebted to the past.

And whatever we can accomplish in the way of love, is paying off our debt for the fact that we can exist.

The impulse toward love grows with the higher ascent of man; wisdom alone is not sufficient.

We do not perfect ourselves through our deeds of love—only through other deeds—but the world is richer for our deeds of love.

God is full of love, is pure love, and is, so to speak, born out of the very substance of love. God is pure, clear love—not the highest wisdom, not the highest power.

If we seek for the source of all creativity, then we come to love; the source of everything living is love.

True love is not capable of diminishment or enhancement; love is something that has a totally different nature than wisdom or power.

Let us suppose that some person knows nothing of the name of Christ Jesus, nothing of what the Gospels tell—but that he does have knowledge of the radical difference between wisdom and power on the one hand, and love on the other. Such a person, even if he knows nothing of the Mystery of Golgotha, is a Christian in the genuine sense of the word.

Being a Christian means grasping the nature of Love.

Love is necessary for the understanding of the Mystery of Golgotha. Only when love streams into wisdom, and vice versa, does it become possible to understand the Mystery of Golgotha.

From "Between Death and Rebirth in Relation to Cosmic Facts" April 1, 1913, Berlin:

True is the word that Leonardo da Vinci said: "Great love is the daughter of great knowledge." And whoever is not willing to do the work of knowledge, he also does not learn, in the true sense, to love. The important things in life are these: that mutual relationships come into existence from man to man.

From "What the Goetheanum Wants and Anthroposophy Should Do" April 23, 1923, Dornach:

One must indeed lose one's earthly ego, in order to bring his real true ego into view. And he who would not be able to develop this self-surrender; he can indeed not approach this true ego. One should like to say: the true ego does not wish to be sought, if it is to appear, if it is to reveal itself; and it hides itself, if it is sought for. For it is only found in love. And love is self-surrender of one's own being to the different being. Therefore, the true ego must be found as a strange being.

Other books by René Querido

published by Rudolf Steiner College Press

Creativity in Education:
The Waldorf Approach

The Esoteric Background of Waldorf Education:
The Cosmic Christ Impulse

Geography and Man's Responsibility for the Earth

The Golden Age of Chartres:
The Teachings of a Mystery School and the Eternal Feminine

The Mystery of the Holy Grail:
A Modern Path of Initiation

Questions and Answers
on Reincarnation and Karma

The Wonder of Childhood:
Stepping into Life

with Hilmar Moore
Behold I Make All Things New:
Toward a World Pentecost